© 1999 Algrove Publishing Limited
ALL RIGHTS RESERVED.
No part of this book may be reproduced in any form, including photocopying,
without permission in writing from the publishers, except by a reviewer who
may quote brief passages in a magazine or newspaper or on radio or television.

Algrove Publishing Limited
36 Mill Street
Almonte, Ontario
Canada K0A 1A0

Telephone: (613) 256-030
Fax: (613) 256-0360
Email: sales@algrove.com

Canadian Cataloguing in Publication Data

Windsor, H. H. (Henry Haven), 1859-1924
    Mission furniture

(Classic reprint series)
Reprint of 3 part set published: Chicago : Popular Mechanics, 1909-1912.
Includes indexes.
ISBN 0-921335-90-3

    1. Furniture making--Amateurs' manuals. 2. Furniture, Mission. I. Title.
II. Series: Classic reprint series (Almonte, Ont.)

TT195.W55 1999   684.1'04   C99-900867-6

Printed in Canada
#60903

Publisher's Note

The three original books by H. H. Windsor were published in 1909, 1910, and 1912. This combined volume has very little repetitive material in it. Obviously the first book was so popular that the author decided to broaden the range to better penetrate the market. The resulting material is as generally applicable today as it was when first printed.

Leonard G. Lee, Publisher
Ottawa
September, 1999

MISSION FURNITURE
HOW TO MAKE IT
PART I

POPULAR MECHANICS HANDBOOKS

CHICAGO
POPULAR MECHANICS CO.

THIS book is one of the series of Handbooks on industrial subjects being published by the Popular Mechanics Company.

Like Popular Mechanics Magazine, and like the other books in this series, it is "written so you can understand it."

The purpose of Popular Mechanics Handbooks is to supply a growing demand for high-class, up-to-date and accurate text-books, suitable for home study as well as for class use, on all mechanical subjects.

The text and illustrations, in each instance, have been prepared expressly for this series by well known experts, and revised by the editor of Popular Mechanics.

HOME-MADE MISSION CHAIR

A mission chair suitable for the dining room can be made from any one of the furniture woods to match the other articles of furniture. The materials

Suitable for Dining Room Use

can be secured from the planing mill dressed and sandpapered ready to cut the tenons and mortises. The material list can be made up from the dimensions given in the detail drawing. The front legs or

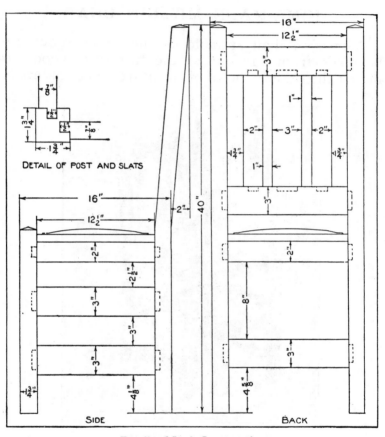

Details of Chair Construction

posts, as well as the back ones, are made from 1¾-in. square stock, the back ones having a slope of 2 in. from the seat to the top. All the slats are made from ⅞-in. material and of such widths as are shown in the detail. The three upright slats in the back are ¾-in. material. The detail drawing shows the side and back, the front being the same as the back from the seat down. All joints are mortised in the posts, as shown. The joints, however, can be made with dowels if desired. If making dowel joints they must be clamped very tight when glued and put together. The seat can be made from one piece of ⅞-in. material, fitted with notches around the posts. This is then upholstered with leather without using springs. Leather must be selected as to color to suit the kind of wood used in making the chair. The seat can also be made with an open center for a cane bottom by making a square of four pieces of ⅞-in. material about 4 in. wide. These pieces are fitted neatly to the proper size and dowelled firmly together. After the cane is put in the opening the cane is covered over and upholstered with leather in the same manner as with a solid bottom.

HOW TO MAKE A LAMP STAND AND SHADE

A library light stand of pleasing design and easy construction is made as follows: Square up a piece of white oak so that it shall have a width and thickness of 1¾ in. with a length of 13 in. Square up two pieces of the same kind of material to the same width and thickness, but with a length of 12 in. each. Square up two pieces to a width and length of 3 in. each with a thickness of 1⅛ in.

If a planing mill is near, time and patience will be saved by ordering one piece 1¾ in. square and 40 in. long, two pieces 1⅛ in. thick and 3 in. square, all planed and sandpapered on all surfaces. The long piece can then be cut at home to the lengths specified above.

The 13-in. piece is for the upright and should have a ½-in. hole bored the full length through the center. If the bit is not long enough to reach entirely through, bore from each end, then use a red-hot iron to finish. This hole is for the electric wire or gas pipe if gas is used.

The two pieces for the base are alike except the groove of one is cut from the top and of the other from the under side, as shown. Shape the under sides first. This can best be done by placing the two pieces in a vise, under sides together, and boring two holes with a 1-in. bit. The center of each hole will be 2½ in. from either end and in the crack between the pieces. The pieces can then be taken out, lines gauged on each side of each, and the wood be-

The Completed Lamp

tween the holes removed with turning saw and scraper steel.

The width of the grooves must be determined by laying one piece upon the other; a trysquare should be used to square the lines across the pieces; however, gauge for depth, gauging both pieces from their top surfaces. Chisel out the grooves and round off the corners as shown in the sketch, using a ¾-in. radius.

These parts may be put together and fastened to the upright by means of two long screws from the under side, placed to either side of the ½-in. hole. This hole must be continued through the pieces forming the base.

The braces are easiest made by taking the two pieces which were planed to 1⅛ in. thick and 3 in. square and drawing a diagonal on each. Find the middle of this diagonal by drawing the central portion of the other diagonal; at this point place the spur of the bit and bore a 1-in. hole in each block.

Saw the two blocks apart, sawing along a diagonal of each. Plane the surfaces on the saw cut smooth and sandpaper the curve made by the bit. Fasten the braces in place by means of roundhead blued screws.

To make a shade such as is shown in the illustration is rather difficult. The shade is made of wood glued up and has art glass fitted in rabbets cut on the inner edges. Such shades can be purchased ready to attach. The sketch shows one method of attaching. Four small pieces of strap iron are bent to the shape shown and fastened to the four sides of the upright. Electric globes—two, three or four may be attached as shown.

The kind of wood finish for the stand will depend upon the finish on the wooden shade, if shade is purchased. Brown Flemish is obtained by first staining the wood with Flemish water stain diluted by the

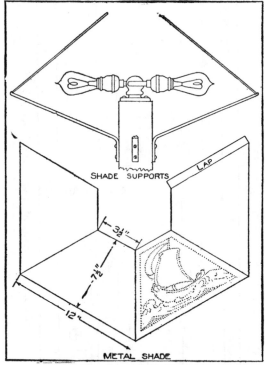

Construction of Shade

addition of two parts water to one part stain. When this is dry, sandpaper the "whiskers" which were raised by the water and fill with a medium dark filler. Directions will be found on the filler cans. When filler has hardened, apply two coats of wax.

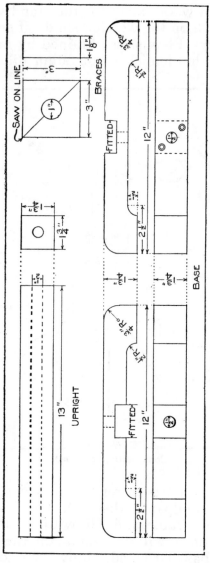

Details of Construction of Library Lamp Stand

The metal shade as shown in the sketch is a "lay-out" for a copper or brass shade of a size suitable for this particular lamp. Such shades are frequently made from one piece of sheet metal and designs are pierced in them as suggested in the "layout." This piercing is done by driving the point of a nail through the metal from the under side before the parts are soldered or riveted together. If the parts are to be riveted, enough additional metal must be left on the last panel to allow for a lap. No lap is needed when joints are soldered.

A better way, and one which will permit the use of heavier metal, is to cut each side of the shade separately and fasten them together by riveting a piece of metal over each joint. The shape of this piece can be made so as to accentuate the rivet heads and thus give a pleasing effect.

For art-glass the metal panels are cut out, the glass is inserted from the under side and held in place by small clips soldered to the frame of the shade.

Pleasing effects are obtained by using one kind of metal, as brass, and reinforcing and riveting with another metal, such as copper.

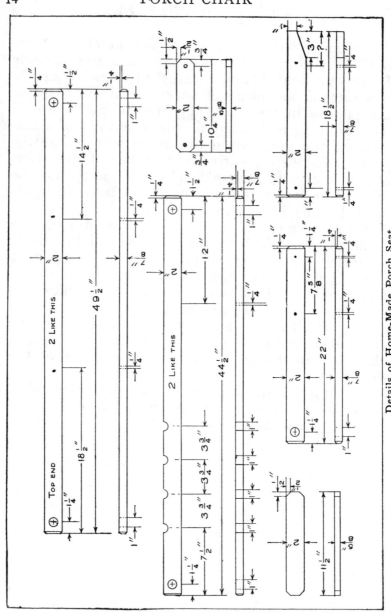

Details of Home-Made Porch Seat

HOW TO MAKE A PORCH CHAIR

The illustration shows a very comfortable and attractive porch chair that can be made with few tools and easily procured material. Most any kind of wood will answer, says the American Carpenter and Builder, but if open grained wood, such as oak or chestnut, is used, the parts should be filled with a paste filler. If the natural color of the wood is not desired, the wood may first be stained, the filler being colored somewhat darker than the stain.

Procure enough lumber to make all the pieces shown in the detail drawing and finish to the dimensions shown, being careful to make the corresponding pieces exactly alike in order to preserve the perfect symmetry which is necessary in work of this kind. In boring the holes care must be taken to keep both edges of the holes sharp and clean. The holes should each be bored until the spur shows; the bit should then be withdrawn and the rest of the boring be done from the other side. The semicircular notches are made by placing the two pieces edge to edge in the vise and placing the spur of the bit in the crack. The 1-in. bit is used. As it will be difficult to finish the boring of these blocks from the second side, the parts remaining may be cut out with the knife after the pieces have been separated.

Five ½-in. dowel rods are needed. It is possible to get these in one long piece if you happen to live near a mill and then all you will have to do is to saw off the desired lengths. However, if they cannot be got easily you can make your own. Two rods each 18¼ in. long; two rods each 20¼ in. and one rod 22¼ in. give the exact lengths. It is well to cut each piece a little longer than required so that the ends which are imperfectly formed may be cut

Porch Chair Finished

off. These rods should fit tight and may be fastened in addition with a small screw or nail from the under or back side.

The hand rests should be nailed to the arms with small nails or brads before the arms are bolted. The illustration of the assembled chair shows the relative position.

The bolts should be ¼ in. and of the following lengths: 4 bolts 2¼ in. long; 2 bolts 2 in. long; 2 bolts 3 in. long. Washers should be placed between adjacent pieces of wood fastened together with bolts and also at both ends of the bolts. This will require 26 washers in all. While the size of the chair may be varied, it will be necessary to keep the proportions if the parts are to fold properly.

HOW TO MAKE A TABOURET

Secure from the planing mill the following pieces and have them planed and sandpapered on two surfaces: For the top, one piece ⅞ in. thick and 17 in. square. For the legs, four pieces ⅞ in. thick, 4¾ in. wide and 18½ in. long. For the lower stretchers, two pieces ⅞ in. thick, 2¾ in. wide and 15¾ in. long. For the top stretchers, two pieces ⅞ in. thick, 2¼ in. wide and 13¼ in. long. No stock need be ordered for the keys, as they can be made out of the waste pieces remaining after the legs are shaped.

Begin work on the four legs first. While both sides of each leg slope, it will be necessary to plane a joint edge on each leg from which to lay out the mortises, grooves and to test the ends. It will be necessary to have a bevel square to use in marking off the slopes and for testing them. To get the setting for the bevel square, make a full sized "lay out" or drawing of the necessary lines in their proper relation to one another and adjust the bevel to those lines.

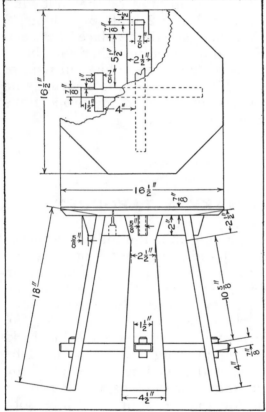

Details of Tabouret

From the joint edge lay out the mortises, grooves and the slopes of s i d e s and e n d s of the legs. Cut the mortises a n d grooves first, then shape up the sides. Saw the sides accurately and quite close to the lines, finishing with the steel cabinet scraper.

Next make the bottom stretchers. In laying out the cross lap joint, the working faces are both to be up when the joint is completed, therefore lay off one groove on the face of one piece and on the side opposite the face on the other. In gauging for depth, however, be careful to keep the gauge block against the working face of each piece.

In laying out the mortises for the keys, the opening on the top surface is to be made ⅛ in. longer than on the under surface. The slope of the key will therefore be ⅛ in. of slope to each ⅞ in. of length. The drawing shows the mortise as ⅞ in. from the shoulders of the tenon. This distance is the same as the thickness of the leg and to insure the key's pulling the shoulder up against the leg firmly, should any of the legs happen to be a little less than ⅞ in., it is well to make the mortise slightly nearer the shoulder than ⅞ in.

It is a good plan to lay out the mortise in the tenon at the same time the shoulders of the tenons are laid out. Otherwise the joint edge being cut off in making the tenon there is no convenient way to locate this mortise accurately.

Lay off the top stretchers according to the dimensions shown in the drawing. Observe the same precautions about the cross lap joint as were given for the lower stretchers, except that the joint edges are to be placed up in this latter case. Make sure the grooves are laid out in the middle before cutting. As a test, place the pieces side by side, examine the markings, then turn one of them end for end and again examine.

The grooves into which the legs pass are ⅛ in. deep and must be very carefully cut. Their purpose is to give rigidity to the tabouret frame. Bore two holes in each stretcher for the screws that are to fasten the top in place.

Make the keys, scrape all the parts and sandpaper those that were not so treated at the mill. Use glue to fasten the tops of the legs to the top stretchers and assemble these parts.

The top is octagonal or eight-sided. To make it, square up a piece to 16½ by 16½ in. Measure the diagonal, take one-half of it and measure from each corner of the board each way along the edges to locate the places at which to cut off the corners. Connect these points, saw and plane the remaining

Tabouret as Completed

four sides. There is to be a ⅝-in. bevel on the under side of the top. Scrape and sandpaper these edges and secure the top to the stretchers with screws. Much time can be saved and a better result obtained if the wood finishing is done before the parts are put together. Especially is this true if stain and filler are used.

A very pretty finish and one easily put on even

after the parts are put together is obtained as follows: Take a barrel and stuff up the cracks or paste paper over them so as to make it as near airtight as possible. In some out-of-the-way place put a dish with about 2 oz. of strong ammonia. Set the tabouret over this dish and quickly invert the barrel over the tabouret. Allow the fumes to act on the wood for at least 15 hours. Remove the barrel and allow the fumes to escape. Polish with several coats of wax such as is used upon floors. Directions for waxing will be found on the cans that contain the wax. This produces the rich nut-brown finish so popular in Arts and Crafts furniture and is known as fumed oak.

HOW TO MAKE A MORRIS CHAIR

The stock necessary to make a morris chair of craftsman design as shown in the engraving can be purchased mill-planed and sandpapered on four sides as given in the following list:

4 posts 1¾ by 3 by 26 in.
2 front and back rails ⅞ by 5½ by 24 in.
2 side rails ⅞ by 5½ by 28 in.
2 arm pieces ⅞ by 5½ by 37 in.
7 slats ⅜ by 2 by 24 in.
2 cleats 1 by 1 by 22½ in.
2 back stiles 1 by 2½ by 24½ in.
2 back rails 1 by 2 by 17 in.
3 back slats ⅜ by 1½ by 19 in.
1 back support ¾ by ¾ by 24 in.
2 support rests 1 by 1½ by 8½ in.
2 dowels ½ in. diameter, 6 in. long.

First make and put together the sides of the chair. While the glue is setting on these parts make and assemble the back. The front and back rails may next be made and placed and the cleats and bottom slats fastened. With the adjustment of the back the chair is ready for the finish.

The posts are to be tenoned on the upper ends. These tenons are to project 3/16 in. above the arm and should be slightly beveled. The lower ends of the posts, likewise, all other projecting ends, should be beveled to avoid their splintering. All sharp corners, as on the arms, should be sandpapered just enough to take their sharpness off, so as not to injure the hand.

That the chair may be properly inclined, the rear posts are cut 1 in. shorter than the forward ones. To get the correct slant on the bottoms of these posts, lay a straightedge so that its edge touches the bottom of the front post at its front surface, but

Complete Morris Chair Without Cushion

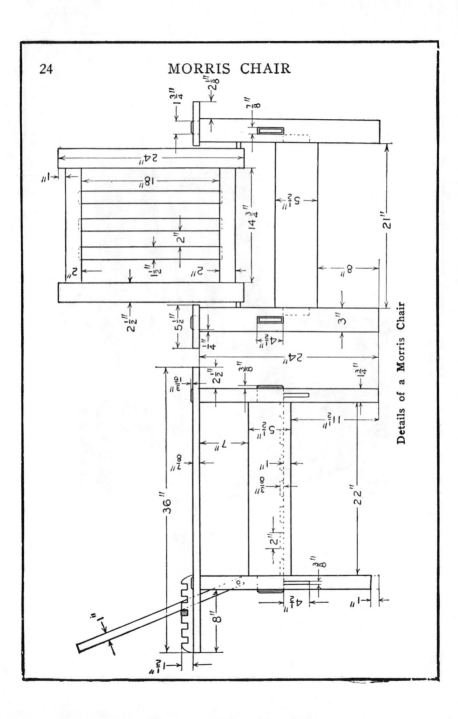

Details of a Morris Chair

keep it 1 in. above the bottom of the rear post. Mark with pencil along the straightedge across both posts.

At the rear ends of the arms are the notched pieces that allow the back to be adjusted to different angles. These pieces may be fastened in place either by means of roundhead screws from above or flatheads from underneath the arms. The notches are to be cut ¾ in. deep. If more than three adjustments are wanted, the arms must be made correspondingly longer.

The dimensions for the tenons on all the larger pieces will be found on the drawing. For the back, the tenons of the cross pieces, the rails, should be ⅜ by 1¼ in. For the slats, the easiest way is to not tenon them but to "let in" the whole end, making the mortises in the rails ⅜ by 1½ in. This will necessitate cutting the sides of the mortises very accurately, but this extra care will be more than compensated by not having to bother with the cutting of tenons on each end of the three back slats.

To finish the chair, put on a coat of water stain, first removing all surplus glue and thoroughly scraping and sandpapering all the parts that were not so treated at the mill. The color of the stain will depend upon the finish desired, whether golden, mission, etc. Water stains cause the grain of the wood to roughen, so it will be necessary to resandpaper the surfaces after the stain has dried, using fine paper. Next apply a coat of filler colored to match the stain. Directions for its application will be found upon the cans in which the filler comes. After the filler has hardened put on a very thin coat of shellac.

What step is taken next will depend upon what kind of a surface is desired. Several coats of polishing wax may be put on. This is easily done—directions will be found on the cans—and makes the most satisfactory finish for mission and craftsman furniture. It is the easiest to apply. Several coats of shellac or of varnish might be put on instead of wax. Each coat of the shellac should be rubbed when thoroughly dried with curled hair or fine steel wool or fine oiled sandpaper. Rub the first coats of varnish with hair-cloth or curled hair and the last coats with pulverized pumice stone and crude oil or raw linseed oil.

Cushions for the chair can be made at home. They may be made of art leather such as Spanish roan skin and the top and bottom parts fastened together by lacing leather thongs through holes previously punched along the edges of the parts. A very pretty effect is obtained by using thongs of a different but harmonious color. The manner of lacing may be any one of the various laces such as are used in lacing belts or as shoestrings. These cushions may be filled with hair or cotton felt. Denim or burlap may also be used as a covering and are much less expensive than the leather. Lace one side and the two ends, then place filling and finish lacing.

Art leather cushions retail at from $16 to $20 a pair and the denim and burlap at $6 to $9.

The bottom cushion should be made the full size of the chair. The front and back rails extend a little above the slats and thus hold it in place. The back cushion will settle down a little and therefore may be made nearly the full length from the slats to the top of the back.

HOME-MADE MISSION BOOK RACK

When making the book rack as shown in the accompanying photograph use quarter-sawed oak if

Light but Strong

possible, as this wood is the most suitable for finishing in the different mission stains. This piece of furniture is very attractive and simple to construct.

The upper shelf can be used for vases or a plant of some kind, while the lower shelves afford ample room for books and magazines.

The slats and legs are fastened to the shelves with 2-in. round-headed brass screws. These can be purchased from any hardware store. One screw is used at each joint of a slat and shelf which calls for 32 screws in all. Holes should be bored into the slats and legs in which to insert the screws. This will keep the wood from splitting. The dimensions are given in the diagram sketch, although these may be changed to suit the requirement of the builder. If no glue is used on the joints when setting up, the rack can easily be taken apart and put in a small bundle for moving.

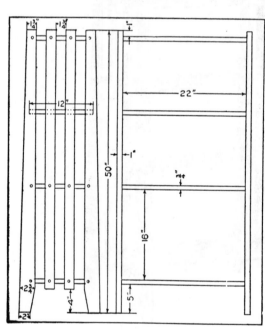

Details of Stand

This Picture is from a Photograph of the Mission Table Described in This Article

HOW TO MAKE A MISSION LIBRARY TABLE

The mission library table, the drawings for which are here given, has been found well proportioned and of pleasing appearance. It can be made of any of the several furniture woods in common use, such as selected, quarter-sawed white oak which will be found exceptionally pleasing in the effect produced.

If a planing mill is at hand the stock can be ordered in such a way as to avoid the hard work of planing and sandpapering. Of course if mill-planed stock cannot be had, the following dimensions must

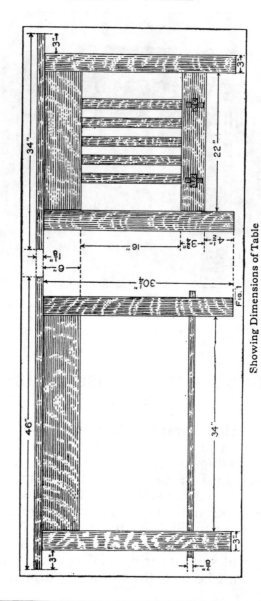

Fig. 1

Showing Dimensions of Table

be enlarged slightly to allow for "squaring up the rough."

For the top, order 1 piece 1⅛ in. thick, 34 in. wide and 46 in. long. Have it S-4-S (surface on four sides) and "squared" to length. Also specify that it be sandpapered on the top surface, the edges and ends.

For the shelf, order 1 piece ⅞ in. thick, 22 in. wide and 42 in. long, with the four sides surfaced, squared and sandpapered the same as for the top.

For the side rails, order 2 pieces ⅞ in. thick, 6 in. wide and 37 in. long, S-4-S and sanded on one side. For the end rails, 2 pieces ⅞ in. thick, 6 in. wide and 25 in. long. Other specifications as for the side rails.

For the stretchers, into which the shelf tenons enter, 2 pieces 1⅛ in. thick, 3¾ in. wide and 25 in. long, surfaced and sanded on four sides. For the slats, 10 pieces ⅝ in. thick, 1½ in. wide and 17 in. long, surfaced and sanded on four sides. For the keys, 4 pieces ¾ in. thick, 1¼ in. wide and 2⅞ in. long, S-4-S. This width is a little wide; it will allow the key to be shaped as desired.

The drawings obviate any necessity for going into detail in the description. Fig. 1 gives an assembly drawing showing the relation of the parts. Fig. 2 gives the detail of an end. The tenons for the side rails are laid off and the mortises placed in the post as are those on the end. Care must be taken, however, not to cut any mortises on the post below, as was done in cutting the stretcher mortises on the ends of the table. A good plan is to set the posts upright in the positions they are to occupy relative to one another and mark with pencil the approximate positions of the mortises. The legs can then

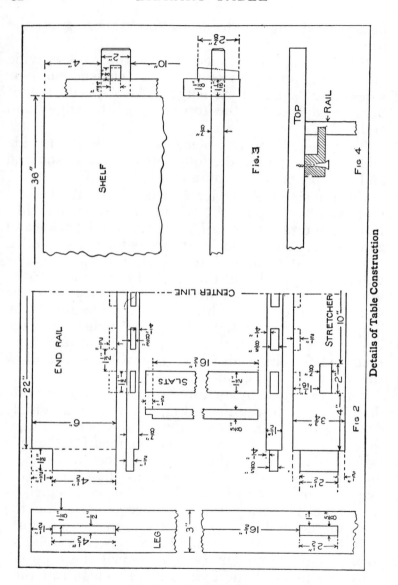

Details of Table Construction

be laid flat and the mortises accurately marked out with a fair degree of assurance that they will not be cut where they are not wanted and that the legs shall "pair" properly when effort is made to assemble the parts of the table.

The table ends should be glued up first and the glue allowed to harden, after which the tenons of the shelf may be inserted and the side rails placed.

There is a reason for the shape, size and location of each tenon or mortise. For illustration, the shape of the tenon on the top rails permits the surface of the rail to extend almost flush with the surface of the post at the same time permitting the mortise in the post to be kept away from that surface. Again, the shape of the ends of the slats is such that, though they may vary slightly in length, the fitting of the joints will not be affected. Care must be taken in cutting the mortises to keep their sides clean and sharp and to size.

In making the mortises for the keyed tenons, the length of mortise must be slightly in excess of the width of the tenon—about ⅛ in. of play to each side of each tenon. With a shelf of the width specified for this table, if such allowance is not made so that the tenons may move sideways, the shrinkage would split the shelf.

In cutting across the ends of the shelf, between the tenons, leave a hole in the waste so that the turning saw or compass saw can be inserted. Saw within one-sixteenth of the line, after which this margin may be removed with chisel and mallet.

In Fig. 3 is shown two views of the keyed tenon and the key. The mortise for the key is to be placed in the middle of the tenon. It will be noted that this mortise is laid out 1 1/16 in. from the shoulder of the tenon while the stretcher is 1⅛ in. thick. This is to insure the key's pulling the shelf tightly against the side of the stretcher.

Keys may be made in a variety of shapes. The one shown is simple and structurally good. Whatever shape is used, the important thing to keep in mind is that the size of the key and the slant of its forward surface where it passes through the tenon must be kept the same as the mortise made for it in the tenon.

The top is to be fastened to the rails by means either of wooden buttons, Fig. 4, or small angle irons.

There are a bewildering number of mission finishes upon the market. A very satisfactory one is obtained by applying a coat of brown Flemish water stain, diluted by the addition of water in the proportion of two parts water to 1 part stain. When this has dried, sand with No. 00 paper, being careful not to "cut through." Next, apply a coat of dark brown filler; the directions for doing this will be found upon the can in which the filler is bought. One coat usually suffices. However, if an especially smooth surface is desired, a second coat may be applied in a similar manner.

After the filler has hardened, a very thin coat of shellac is to be put on. When this has dried, it should be sanded lightly and then one or two coats of wax should be properly applied and polished. Directions for waxing are upon the cans in which the wax is bought. A beautiful dull gloss so much sought by finishers of modern furniture will be the result of carefully following these directions.

HOME-MADE MISSION CANDLESTICK

There are many kinds of mission candlesticks, but few of them carry out the mission design throughout. Herewith is illustrated a candlestick which may be made from the various woods that will have the style and lines of mission craft work. The base is made from 1-in. material, 4½ in. square. Two holes are bored and countersunk for screws to hold the post and handle. The post is 2¼ in. high, bored in one end to fit the size of a candle. The post is covered with a ⅜-in. thick cap, 2 in. square. This, also, is bored to fit the candle. The handle is ⅜ in. thick and 3 in. long with a ⅜-in. square mortise and is notched to fit the base. The wood may be selected to match any other piece of furniture and finished in any of the mission stains.

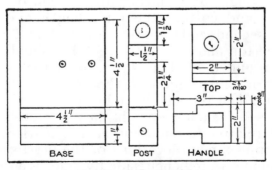

Details of Candlestick

ANOTHER STYLE OF MISSION CHAIR

The material necessary to make a mission chair as shown in the accompanying illustration may be secured from a planing mill with all four surfaces squared and sandpapered. The mill can do this work quickly and the expense will be nothing compared with the time it takes to do the work by hand. The following is the stock list:

```
4 legs, 2½ by 2½ by 32½ in.
2 bottom end rails ⅞ by 5¾ by 23½ in.
2 bottom side rails ⅞ by 5¾ by 28½ in.
2 top end rails ⅞ by 4½ by 23½ in.
1 top back rail ⅞ by 4½ by 28½ in.
2 cleats ⅞ by 2½ by 26½ in.
7 slats ½ by 2 by 24 in.
```

This design was purposely made simple. If it is considered too severe and the worker has had some experience in woodwork, it can easily be modified by adding vertical slats in back and sides. These should be made of ½-in. stock and their ends should be "let into" the rails by means of mortises.

Either plain red oak or quarter-sawed white oak will do. Begin by squaring up one end of each leg, marking and cutting them to length and planing up the second ends so that they shall be square. Both the top and bottom of each leg should be beveled or rounded off about ¼ in. so that they may not splinter or cause injury to the hand.

When all of the legs have been made of the same length, set them on end in the positions they are to have relative to one another and mark with pencil the approximate locations of the mortises. Next, place them on the bench, side by side, even the ends

Mission Chair Complete

and square sharp lines across to indicate the ends of the mortises. The drawing shows the dimensions to use. A sharp pencil should be used for this marking and the lines should be carried entirely across the two faces of each piece.

Set the gauge for the side of the mortise nearest the face edge. With this setting, mark all the mortises, then set for the second side of the mortise and complete the gauging.

There are two ways of cutting small mortises in common use. One is by using a chisel of a width just equal to that of the mortise. The other is by using a smaller chisel after the mortise has first been bored with the brace and bit. In the first method the cutting is begun at the middle of the mortise where a V-shaped opening is made the full depth of the mortise that is to be. Continuing from the middle, vertical cuts are taken first toward one end and then toward the other. The chips are pried out as the cutting proceeds. In making the last cut this prying must be omitted, otherwise the edge of the mortise would be ruined. It will be necessary to stand so as to look along the opening in order to get the sides plumb.

This method of cutting, when once the "knack" has been attained, will be found much easier, quicker and more accurate for small openings, such as these, than the usual method. The second method, which is the usual one, needs no description.

The rails should next have the tenons cut on their ends. It may not be out of place to remind the amateur that the lengths of the various like pieces can best be laid off by placing them on the bench, measuring off the proper distances on one of

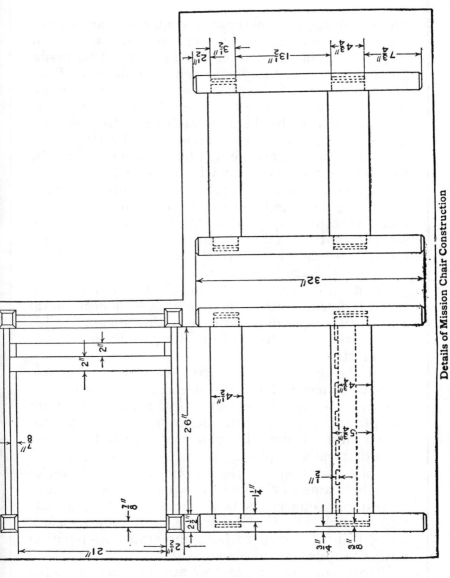

Details of Mission Chair Construction

them and then with trysquare marking across the edges of all of them at once. This not only saves time in that but one set of measurements need be made, but it insures all the pieces being similarly laid off. In measuring off for the shoulders of the tenons, begin at the middle of the length of the rail and measure half of the distance each way. By doing so, if there are any slight differences in the lengths of the pieces this difference will be divided between the two tenons and no harm will be done.

In gauging the tenons take the precaution to mark a working face and joint edge, even if all the surfaces were finish-planed at the mill. It is very important that all tenon gauging be done from these faces. The same is true of the legs or posts, and the slats if there are to be any.

To avoid confusion it is well to number each tenon by means of the chisel with a Roman numeral and its corresponding mortise with the same. This will prevent the fitting of one tenon into more than one mortise.

Put the parts together with warm glue if it can be had, otherwise use the prepared cold glue. In cold weather the wood ought to be warmed before the glue is applied. Put the ends of the chair together first. When the glue has set on these put the other rails in place.

When clamping up the second set of rails make sure the frame of the chair is square. The best way to test for squareness is to measure the diagonals with a stick. Spring the frame until they measure alike, using a brace to hold the frame in position until the glue can harden.

Before staining, scrape off any surplus glue, for

stain will not adhere to glue and a white spot will be the result of failing to remove it. Fasten cleats to the front and back rails with screws. To these cleats fasten the slats as shown in the drawing. A cushion of Spanish leather, such as is shown in the photograph, can be bought at the furniture store or the upholsterer's. It can be made by the amateur quite easily, however. The two parts are fastened together with leather thongs and the filling is of hair or elastic felt. A cushion for the back might well be provided.

To finish the wood to match a brown leather proceed as follows: With a cloth or brush, stain the wood with brown Flemish water stain diluted by the addition of four parts of water. When this has dried, sandpaper smooth, using No. 00 paper held on the tips of the fingers. Apply a dark brown filler. When this has flatted, i. e., when the gloss has disappeared, which will be in the course of ten or fifteen minutes, wipe off clean with excelsior and then with waste or a cloth. Allow this to dry over night, then apply two or three coats of wax. Polish each coat with a flannel cloth by briskly rubbing it.

A settle can be made after this design by using longer front and back rails. Rails 42 in. between shoulders will make a good length for a settle.

HOW TO MAKE AND FINISH A MAGAZINE STAND

For the magazine stand shown herewith there will be needed the following pieces:

1 top, ⅞ in. by 15½ in. by 16½ in.
1 shelf, ⅞ in. by 11½ in. by 12½ in.
1 shelf, ⅞ in. by 12½ in. by 14¾ in.
1 shelf, ⅞ in. by 13½ in. by 16½ in.
2 sides, ⅞ in. by 14½ in. by 33½ in.
1 brace, ⅞ in. by 3¼ in. by 17 in.
1 brace, ⅞ in. by 2½ in. by 11½ in.
6 braces, ⅞ in. by 2 in. by 2 in.

Order these pieces mill-planed on two surfaces to the thickness specified above and also sandpapered. Quarter-sawed white oak makes the best appearance of all the woods that are comparatively easy to obtain. Plain sawed red or white oak will look well but are more liable to warp than the quarter-sawed. This is quite an element in pieces as wide as these.

Begin work on the sides first. Plane a joint edge on each and from this work the two ends. The ends will be square to the joint edge but beveled to the working face. A bevel square will be needed for testing these beveled ends.

To set the bevel make a drawing, full size or nearly so, of the front view and place the bevel on the drawing, adjusting its sides to the angle wanted. Work from a center line in laying off the drawing.

Having planed the ends, lay off the sides. This is done by measuring from the joint edge along the bottom 14 in., from the joint edge along the top 1½ in. and from this 11 in. Connect the points by means of a pencil and straightedge.

Completed Stand

Before cutting off the joint edges of the pieces measure off and square lines across to indicate the locations of the shelves. Put both pieces together and mark across both joint edges at once to insure getting both laid off alike.

The design at the bottom can be varied to suit the fancy of the worker. For such a design as is shown, draw on paper, full size, half of it; fold on the center line and with scissors cut both sides of the outline by cutting along the line just drawn. Trace around this pattern on the wood, and saw out with compass or turning saw.

The shelves may now be made. The bevel of the ends of the shelves will be the same as for the ends of the side pieces. The lengths may be obtained by measuring the drawing. Remember that length is always measured along the grain and that the end grain of the shelves must extend from side to side in this stand. The widths may be obtained by measuring the width of the sides at the points marked out on them for the location of the shelf ends. It is best not to have the shelves the full width of the sides, since the edges of the shelves are to be faced with leather. Make each shelf ½ in. less than the width of the side, at the place that the shelf is to be fastened.

The top will be squared up in the usual manner, 15 in. wide by 16 in. long.

These parts may now be put together. They may be fastened in any one of a variety of ways. Round-head blued screws may be placed at regular intervals through the sides. Finishing nails may be used and the heads set and covered with putty stained to match the wood. Finish nails may be placed at regular intervals and fancy headed nails used to cover the heads.

The braces should be formed and fitted but not fastened until the finish has been applied. Thor-

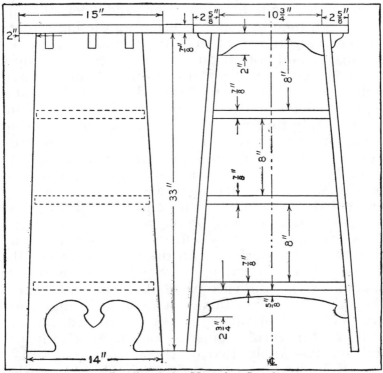

Details of the Magazine Stand

oughly scrape and sandpaper all parts not already so treated. Probably no other finish appeals to so many people as golden oak. There is no fixed standard of color for golden oak. Different manufacturers have set standards in their part of the country, but the prevailing idea of golden oak is usually that of a rich reddish brown.

Proceed as follows: Egg shell gloss: 1.—One coat of golden oak water stain, diluted with water if a light golden is desired. 2.—Allow time to dry, then sandpaper lightly with fine sandpaper. This is to smooth the grain and to bring up the high lights by removing the stain from the wood. Use No. 00 sandpaper and hold it on the finger tips. 3.—Apply a second coat of the stain diluted about one-half with water. This will throw the grain into still higher relief and thus produce a still greater contrast. Apply this coat of stain very sparingly, using a rag. Should this stain raise the grain, again rub lightly with fine worn sandpaper, just enough to smooth. 4.—When this has dried, put on a light coat of thin shellac. Shellac precedes filling that it may prevent the high lights—the solid parts of the wood —from being discolored by the stain in the filler, and thus causing a muddy effect. The shellac being thin does not interfere with the filler's entering the pores of the open grain. 5.—Sand lightly with fine sandpaper. 6.—Fill with paste filler colored to match the stain. 7.—Cover this with a coat of orange shellac. This coat of shellac might be omitted, but another coat of varnish must be added. 8.—Sandpaper lightly. 9.—Apply two or three coats of varnish. 10.—Rub the first coats with hair cloth or curled hair and then with pulverized pumice stone, crude oil or linseed oil. Affix the braces just after filling, using brads and puttying the holes with putty colored to match the filler. The shelves may be faced with thin leather harmonizing with the oak, ornamental headed tacks being used to fasten it in place.

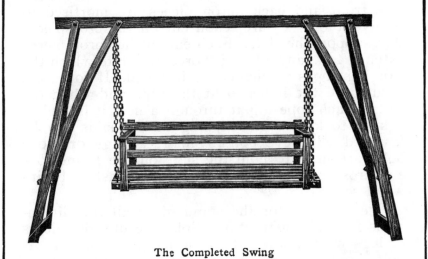

The Completed Swing

HOME-MADE LAWN SWING

The coming of spring and summer calls forth various kinds of porch and lawn furniture. A porch or lawn swing to accommodate two or more persons is a thing desired by most people. The lawn swing as shown in the picture is portable and does not need stakes to hold it to the ground. While this swing is substantial and rigid it can be moved from place to place on the lawn, or the chains can be fastened with heavy hooks to the ceiling of a porch instead of using the stand. Either ropes or chains may be used to hang the swing and should be of such length that the seat will be about 20 in. from the ground or floor.

The drawing giving the dimensions for constructing the seat shows how the parts are put together. The front and back apron pieces are mortised to receive a 1-in. square tenon cut on the crosspieces that support the slats. Each end of the apron pieces extends 4 in., and a hole is bored at A into which the hanging ropes or chains are fastened. If ropes are used, bore the holes to fit the rope and when the end of each rope is put through a hole it is tied in a knot to keep from slipping out. Chains can be fastened with eye bolts. Small carriage or stove bolts are used to hold the slats on the framework and cross pieces. The arm rests are fastened with wood screws.

The drawing for the stand gives all the dimensions for its construction. Split the upright pieces or legs with a saw cut to the length as shown. A bolt should be put through each piece edgewise at the end of the saw cut, to keep the wood from splitting any farther when the ends are spread to receive the bolts through the cross pieces at the top. The upper ends of the ropes or chains are fastened close to and under the bolt holding the inside forks of the uprights. This bolt can be long enough

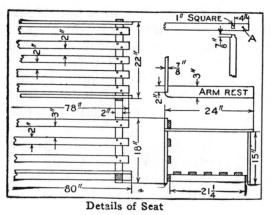

Details of Seat

to fasten a clevis that will hang underneath for this purpose. The whole swing can be painted with a forest green color which is very suitable for summer outdoor furniture.

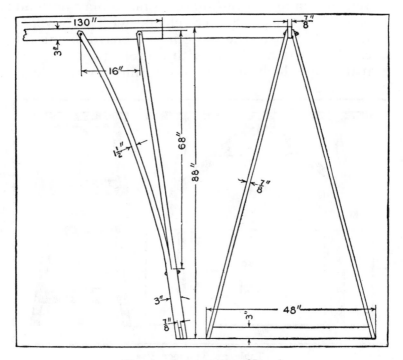

Showing Construction of Stand

HOW TO MAKE A PORTABLE TABLE

A table for outdoor use that can be taken apart, stored or changed from place to place may be made at small expense. Fasten cleats with screws, as shown in Fig. 1, to the bottom of a board of suitable size. The legs are built with a cross piece, A, Fig. 4, at the top which fits into slot formed by the cleats,

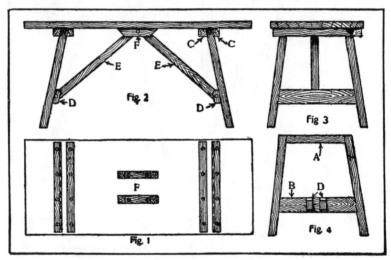

Table for Outdoor Use

CC, and a crosspiece, B, that has two cleats, D, making a place to receive the bottom end of the brace, E, Fig. 2. The upper ends of the braces, EE, fit in between two pieces, F, fastened in the middle of the board. The three pins fitting loosely in DD and F, Fig. 2, are all that holds table together. The end view is shown in Fig. 3.

HOW TO MAKE A COMBINATION BIL-LIARD TABLE AND DAVENPORT

A small size billiard table which can be converted quickly into a davenport is made as follows: Secure clear, selected plain sawed white oak in sizes as indicated by the drawing. Have these planed at the mill to the widths and thicknesses specified.

The lower part should be made first. Cut the four posts to length, chamfering the ends somewhat so that they will not splinter when in use. Lay out and cut the mortises which are to receive the rails. The lower rails are to be $1\frac{1}{8}$ in. thick and the mortises are to be laid out in the legs so as to bring their outer surfaces almost flush with those of the posts. The upper rails are $2\frac{1}{4}$ in. wide. The slats are $\frac{3}{4}$ in. thick. Tenons should be thoroughly pinned to the sides of the mortises as shown in the illustration. The braces are $1\frac{3}{4}$ in. thick and are fastened to place with roundhead screws and glue.

The seat may be made by putting in a solid bottom that shall rest upon cleats fastened to the inner surfaces of the rails. The top of this bottom should rest about $\frac{3}{4}$ in. below the top edge of the rails. A well filled leather cushion completes this part.

A more satisfactory result is obtained by putting in springs and upholstering the seat. Upon this the leather cushion can be placed.

The top or table is built upon and about a heavy frame of well seasoned $1\frac{3}{4}$-in. by $5\frac{3}{4}$-in. white pine. The parts to this frame are thoroughly mortised and tenoned together. Middle stretchers, lengthwise and

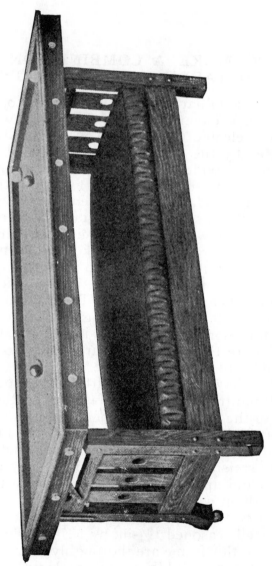

By Swinging the Top Back the Table is Transformed into the Elegant Davenport Seen on the Opposite Page

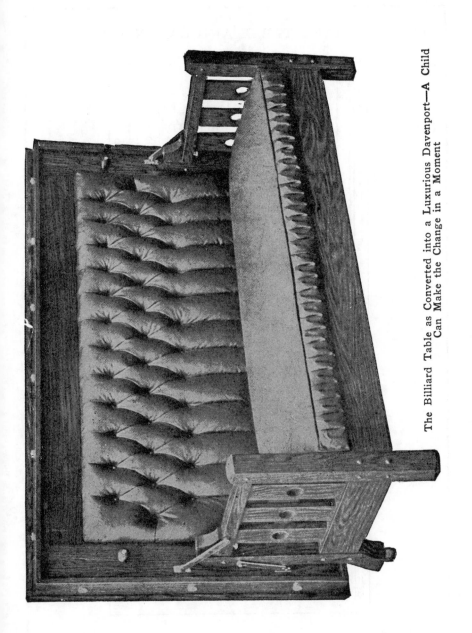

The Billiard Table as Converted into a Luxurious Davenport—A Child Can Make the Change in a Moment

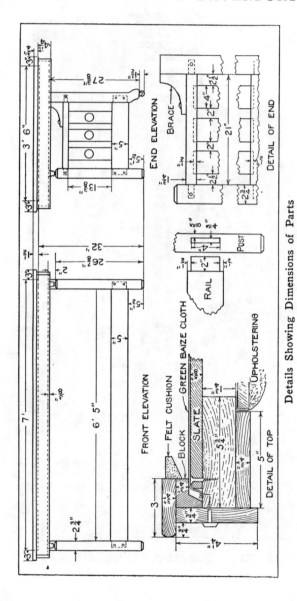

Details Showing Dimensions of Parts

crosswise, give added strength and rigidity. Upon this frame the slate bed is leveled by planing the frame wherever necessary. Slats are fastened to the bed by screws, the heads of which are countersunk so that they may be covered over even with plaster of paris.

The top and side facings are built together, the angle being reinforced with block and glue, as shown in detail. These facings, to which the cushions are attached, are afterward made fast to the frame by ornamental headed screws. The detail and photograph show the manner of applying the under facing.

Before attaching the top and side facings, the bed cloth should be placed over the slate and fastened. The nap of the cloth should run from the head toward the opposite end of the table. Draw the cloth as tight as possible, taking care that there shall be no wrinkles.

The billiard cushions can be bought ready to cover. The bumpers which keep the top from striking the front posts can be obtained by making proper selection from oak door bumpers carried in stock by hardware dealers. The brass swing bars, most likely, can be obtained at the same place.

The upholstering on the under side of the top— the back of the davenport—is to be built upon a stout frame made of some suitable common wood, and the whole set in the recess formed as shown in the detail drawing—the whole being fastened from the back before the slate bed is put in position.

Effort should be made to select leather of a color that will harmonize with the wood finish which is to be applied.

EASILY MADE BOOK SHELVES

Very cheap but useful and attractive book shelves are shown in the accompanying drawing. The verti-

cal strips, A, may be ¾ in. by 2 in. and are screwed to four shelves, B, each cut to the shape of a quarter circle. The screws are all countersunk and as the heads all come on the side next to the wall, they do not show. The design might be varied somewhat to suit the fancy of the builder, although the appearance of the shelves constructed as shown is very pleasing, especially so if the workmanship is good and the wood carefully stained and varnished. The total cost of construction was less than 75 cents.

A BLACKING CASE TABOURET

A substantial piece of mission furniture which may be used as a tabouret or plant stand as well as a blacking case, in which there is a receptacle for brushes, blacking and a shoe rest, is shown in the illustration. The stock can be secured millplaned, sandpapered and in lengths almost ready to be assembled. The stock list consists of the following pieces:

4 posts, 1½ by 1½ by 17 in.
4 side rails, 1 by 6½ by 9½ in.
2 top pieces, 1 by 8¼ by 16½ in.
1 bottom, ¼ by 9½ by 9½ in.
1 cleat, 1 by 1 by 18 in.

The posts and cleat are surfaced on four sides, while the other pieces are surfaced on only two sides. The allowance of ½ in. on the side rails, top and bottom, is for fitting the joints. Be sure the surfaces of the pieces for the posts are square and the ends sawed square off, making the posts exactly the same length when they come from the mill.

Square up the four side rails to 6 by 9 in. Cut one end of each post tapering with a chisel; face and sandpaper the posts and side rails before making the joints. The side rails are attached to the posts with three dowels to each joint. The place for each dowel is located by making a line exactly in the middle lengthwise on each end of each side rail. Three lines are made to intersect this middle line, as shown in the detail. Drive a ½-in. brad in each intersection allowing a small portion of each brad to project, and cut off

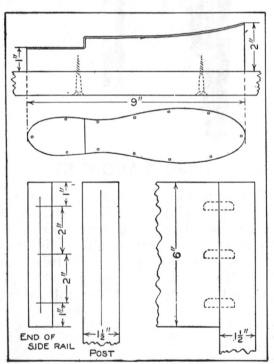

Details of Shoe Rest

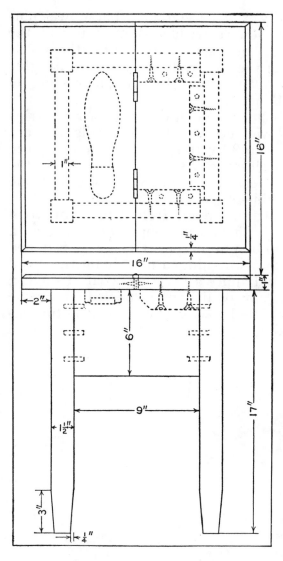

Details of Tabouret Construction

the heads. Gauge a line in the middle of each post at the top where the joints are to be made and press the end of a side rail containing the brads against the post. This will mark the places to bore holes for the dowels. Pull out the brads and bore holes for the dowel pins.

When gluing up the side rails and posts, first put on a coat of glue on the ends of the side rails and let it dry. This will fill up the pores in the end grain of the wood which will make a strong joint when finally glued together.   The dowel pins are made $\frac{3}{8}$ in. square with a slight taper at the ends.   These can be easily forced into the holes, when the ends of the side rails are coated with glue and ready to be put together, by clamps pressing on the outside of the posts.

The bottom is held in position with narrow strips tacked on the lower edge of the side rails. Square up the top pieces to 8 by 16 in. and fasten one piece to the top with cleats and screws as shown in the drawing. The other piece is hinged to the first one with two 2-in. hinges.

The shoe rest can be made from a block of wood and covered with sheet tin, copper or brass, or a cast-iron rest can be purchased. The rest is fastened to the under side of the hinged top. Stain the wood any dark color and apply a very thin coat of shellac. Put on wax and you will have a finish that can be renewed at any time by wiping with a little turpentine and rewaxing.

HOW TO MAKE A ROLL TOP DESK

The Desk Complete

The materials for this roll top desk can be purchased from a mill dressed and sandpapered so the hardest part of the work will be finished. The wood must be selected to suit the builder and to match other articles of furniture. The following list of materials will be required:

```
 68 lineal ft. of  1 by  3   in. hardwood.
 65 lineal ft. of  1 by  2   in. hardwood.
  3 lineal ft. of ¼ by 24    in. hardwood.
 45 lineal ft. of ¼ by 10½   in. hardwood.
 36 lineal ft. of  1 by 12   in. hardwood.
 35 lineal ft. of ⅜ by  9    in. soft wood.
100 sq. ft. of ½ by 12 in. soft wood.
  1 piece 34 in. wide and 54 in. long hardwood.
 30 pieces 1 by 1 in. 48 in. long.
```

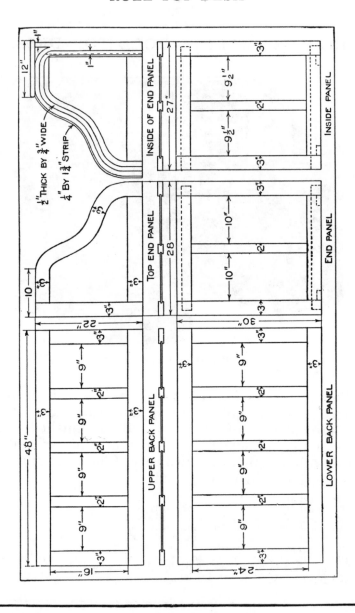

The upper and lower back panels are constructed very similar, the only difference being in the height. The inside edge of the 3-in. pieces is plowed with a ¼-in. plow ⅜ in. deep exactly in the center and also both edges of each 2-in. piece. The 16-in. pieces in the upper back panel and the 24-in. pieces in the lower back panel must be cut ½ in. longer and a ¼-in. tongue made on each end to fit into the plowed groove and form a mortise joint.

The upper back panel is filled in with four boards 9½ in. wide and 16½ in. long, while the four boards in the lower back panel are 9½ in. wide and 24½ in. long cut from the ¼-in. hard wood. When the grooves are cut properly, the joints made perfect and the boards fitted to the right size, these two panels can be assembled and pressed together in cabinet clamps. This will make the outside dimensions as given in the drawing.

The end panels are made very similar to the lower back panel, the only difference being in the width of the filling boards, which are 10½ in. for the outside end panels and 10 in. for the inside panels. One end panel and one inside panel make the sides of one pedestal. As the end panels are 1 in. wider than the inside panels they overlap the back panel and cover up the rough ends of the boards. A 1-in. piece 2 in. wide is fastened at the top and bottom of each end and inside panels as shown by the dotted lines. The lower back panel is fastened on by turning screws through the back and into the ends of these pieces. The bottom pieces have 2-in. notches cut out, as shown, into which to fit two cross-pieces across the bottom of the pedestal for holding the casters. The top end panels are made as shown in the drawing, the inside edge of the pieces being plowed out, making a groove the same size as in the other pieces of the panels. The panel board is cut to the proper shape from the 1/4- by 24-in. material. The length given in the material list will be sufficient if the pointed ends are allowed to pass each other when laying out the design.

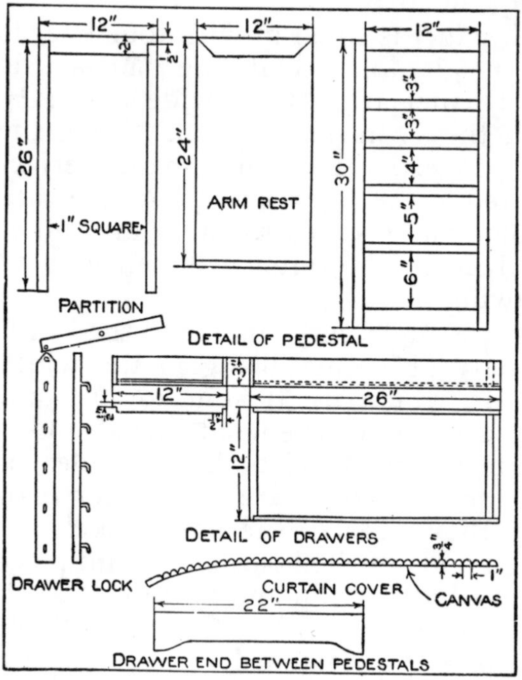

DETAIL OF PEDESTAL

DETAIL OF DRAWERS

DRAWER LOCK

CURTAIN COVER — CANVAS

DRAWER END BETWEEN PEDESTALS

Instead of cutting a groove for the roll top curtain, one is made by fastening a 1/2- by 3/4-in. strip 7/8 in. down from the edge and on the inside of the panel. A thin 1/4- by 1 3/4-in. strip is bent to form the shape of the edge and fastened with round - headed brass screws. A 1-in. piece is fastened at the back and a groove cut into it as shown by the dotted line into which to slide a 1/4-in. back board. The top is a 12-in. board 54 in. long.

As both pedestals are made alike, the detail of

only one is shown. The partitions upon which the drawers slide are made up from 1-in. square material with a 2-in. end fitted as shown. Dimensions are given for the divisions of each drawer, but these can be changed to suit the builder. The detail of one drawer is shown, giving the length and width, the height being that of the top drawer. The roll top curtain is made up from 1-in. pieces ¾ in. thick and 48 in. long, cut in an oval shape on the outside, tacked and glued to a piece of strong canvas on the inside. The end piece is 2 in. wide, into which two lift holes or grooves are cut and a lock attached in the middle of the edge. A drawer lock can be made as shown and attached to the back panel and operated by the back end of the roll top curtain when it is opened and closed.

The top board, which is 34 by 54 in., can be fitted with end pieces as shown or left in one piece with the edges made rounding.

At this point in the construction of the parts they can be put together. The sides of each pedestal are fastened together by screws passed through the 1-in. square pieces forming the partition and into the sides of the panels. When each pedestal is put together the lower back panel is fastened to them with screws turned into the pieces provided as stated in making the end panels. The top board is now adjusted with equal edges projecting and fastened in position with finishing nails. As the top panels cover directly over where the nails are driven, the heads will not show. The upper back panel is fastened to the curved ends and the whole top held to the top board with cast corner brackets that can be purchased at any hardware store. The top

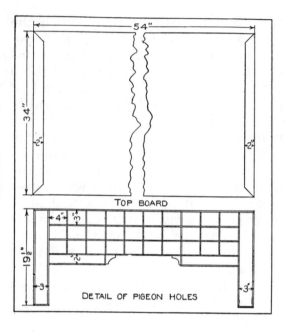

TOP BOARD

DETAIL OF PIGEON HOLES

should not be drawn together too close before the 1/4-in. back board is put in the grooves and the roll top curtain placed in position.

The detail showing the pigeon holes gives sizes for 30 openings 3 by 4 in., two book stalls at the ends, 3 in. wide, and two small drawers. This frame is built up as shown from the 3/8-in. soft wood, and fastened in the back part of the top with small brads.

HOW TO MAKE A ROMAN CHAIR

In making this roman chair, as well as other articles of mission furniture, the materials can be ordered from the mill with much of the hard work completed. Order the stock to make this chair as follows:

    4 posts, 1⅞ by 1⅞ by 30 in.
    2 top rails, ⅞ by 2¾ by 20 in.
    2 bottom rails, ⅞ by 2¼ by 20 in.
    2 rails, ⅞ by 4 by 16 in.
    2 side rails, ⅞ by 4 by 28 in.
    1 stretcher, ⅞ by 3 by 30 in.

Have all these pieces mill planed on the four sides straight and square, also have them sandpapered on the four sides of each. Plain sawed white

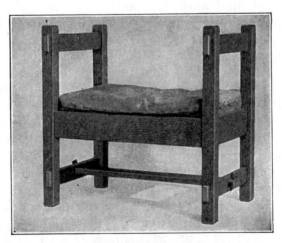

The Roman Chair

or red oak finishes nicely and is easily obtained. The sizes are specified exact as to thickness and width, but the lengths are longer than is needed. This is to allow for cutting and fitting.

Begin by squaring one end of each post; measure the length 28 in. and, placing all of them side by side, square a line across the four, saw, then plane these ends square. The top and bottom side rails are treated in a similar manner, their length being 19⅛ in. each. These pieces extend right through the posts projecting ⅝ in. beyond the surface. The mortises in the posts must be cut smoothly and of exact size. Wood pins fasten these rails and posts together. The other rails have tenons ½ by 3 in. shouldered on the two edges and one side. The mortise in the post is placed central. On the ends of the chair the shouldered side is turned in (see photograph), while on the front and back they are turned out. Miter the ends of these tenons. These tenons are to be glued and clamped—the ends of the chair being put together first. When this is dry the sides are clamped. The stretcher should have its ends shouldered on the two edges so as to make a 2½-in. tenon. Allow the tenons to extend 1⅛ in. beyond the cross rail and cut mortises in these tenons for the keys.

All projecting tenons, as well as the tops and bottoms of the posts, should be chamfered about ⅛ in. For the seat, screw cleats to the insides of the rails and place a platform of thin boards so that its top surface is ½ in. below the top of the rails.

A cushion can be made, as shown in the photograph, by lacing with leather thongs two pieces of Spanish leather cut to proper length and width.

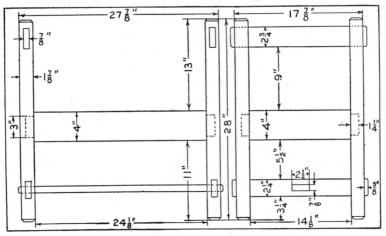

Details of Parts of Chair

When nearly laced fill with any of the common upholsterer's fillings.

For a brown stain, dissolve by boiling in 4 oz. of water, extract of logwood the size of a walnut. Apply hot and repeat until the desired color is obtained. Stains can be bought ready prepared, however, and are quite satisfactory. Finish by applying several coats of wax.

HOW TO MAKE A SETTEE

This handsome piece of mission furniture is designed to be made up in three different pieces as desired, the only changes necessary being in the length of the one front and the two back rails. The settee can be made into a three-cushion length by adding the length of another cushion to the dimensions of the one front and two back rails. A companion piece chair can be made by using suitable length rails to admit only one cushion. The following stock list of materials ordered mill-planed and sandpapered will be sufficient to make up the settee as illustrated. Oak is the most suitable wood which can be finished in either mission or a dark golden oak.

    3 rails 1 by 4 by 52¼ in.
    4 end rails 1 by 4 by 24¼ in.
    4 posts 2¼ in. square by 34½ in.
    13 slats ½ by 5 by 21¼ in.
    2 cleats 1 in. square by 51 in.

All the rails are mortised into the posts for a depth of ⅝ in., also the slats are mortised ⅝ in. into the rails. The material list gives the exact dimensions for the rails and slats as they will not need to be squared for entering the mortises, provided you are careful to get all lengths cut to dimensions. When cutting the mortises take care to get them square and clean. The posts have ½ in. extra added for squaring up and cutting the corners sloping on the top ends.

The joints are all put together with glue. Nails can be driven into the posts intersecting the tenons of the rails on the inside, as they will not show and will help to make the settee more solid.

The cushions can be made with or without springs as desired. If made without springs, 15 slats must be provided in the material list ½ in. thick, 2

A Complete Two-Cushion Settee

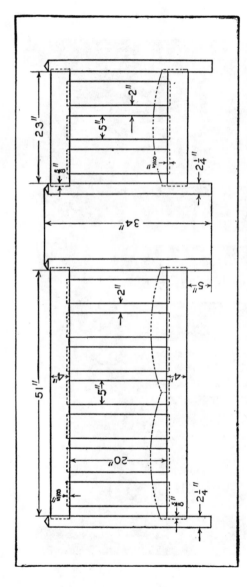

Details of a Mission Settee

in. wide and 24 in. long to be placed on the cleats fastened to the inside of each bottom rail. The two cleats are fastened one on each inside of the front and back rails with screws. The location as to height of these cleats will depend upon the kind of cushions used. The parts necessary to make the cushions with springs are as follows:

    4 pieces 1 by 2½ by 26 in.
    8 pieces 1 by 2½ by 24 in.
    4 pieces 1 by 2½ by 22 in.
    32 8-in. springs.
    2 pieces leather about 29 by 31 in.

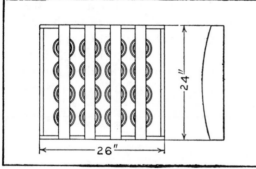

Details of the Cushion

An open box is made from two 26-in. and two 22-in. pieces, and across the bottom are mortised and set in four 24-in. pieces to form slats on which to set the springs. The tops of the springs are tied or anchored with stout cords running in both directions and fastened to the inside of the pieces forming the open box. These should be tied in such manner as to hold each spring so it cannot slip over and come in contact with another spring.

Roan or pebbled leather are very popular for cushions for this style of furniture. The leather is drawn over the springs and tacked to the outside of the open box frame. When complete the cushions are set in loose on the cleats, which should, in this case, be placed about 1 in. from the top of the rails.

HOW TO MAKE A PYROGRAPHER'S TABLE

Any pyrographer will appreciate the construction of the table and cabinet as illustrated. Anyone doing burnt wood work will know the annoyance of building up a steady support for the arm to the level of the article on which the work is to be done. The size of this table may be made to suit the surroundings and the space of the builder. Figure 1 shows the table with a slot cut in the side support in which to place the thumb screw of the bracket as shown on top of the table. It will be noticed, Fig. 2, that while both drawer and cabinet are available for storing the apparatus, they are not in the way of the op-

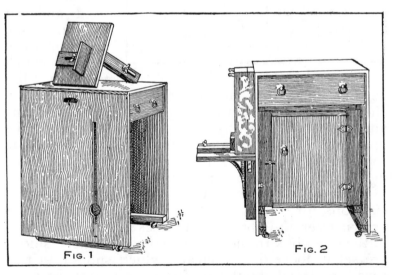

Fig. 1
Fig. 2

Convenient Pyrographer's Table

erator while sitting at his work; the drawer overhangs the knees and the cabinet is far enough back not to interfere with sitting up close to the work. The bracket shelf slides in the slot at the side of the table, and is fastened to any height by the t h u m b s c r e w There is also a smaller slide bracket on the shelf to clamp irregular objects to the side of the t a b l e. The thumb screws, hinges

Fig. 3.

Storage for Apparatus

and drawer pulls can be purchased from any hardware store. When the table is not in use for pyrography it can be used for a writing table or a round top provided and attached on which to play games. When used for this purpose the bracket, as well as the pyrographic outfit, is stowed away in the cabinet as shown in Fig. 3.

MISSION STAINS

What is mission oak stain? There are many on the market, with hardly two alike in tone. The true mission oak stain may be said to show a dull gray, the flakes showing a reddish tint, while the grain of the wood will be almost a dead black. To produce such a stain take 1 lb. of drop black in oil and ½ oz. of rose pink in oil, adding a gill of best japan drier, thinning with three half-pints of turpentine. This will make about 1 qt. of stain. Use these proportions for a larger quantity of stain. Strain it through cheese cloth. Japan colors will give a quicker drying stain than that made with oil colors, and in this case omit the japan and add a little varnish to bind it.

One of the most popular of all the fancy oaks has been that known as Flemish, and this in spite of its very somber color, says Wood Craft. There are several ways of producing Flemish finish; you can fill the wood with a paste filler strained with raw umber, and when dry apply a stain of transparent flat raw umber, and for the darker shades of finish use drop black with the umber. Varnish and rub down.

According to a foreign technical journal, French workmen mahoganize various kinds of woods by the following method: The surface of the wood to be stained is made perfectly smooth. Then it is given a coating of dilute nitric acid which is rubbed well into the wood fiber. Then it is stained with a mixture made by dissolving 1½ oz. of dragon's blood in a pint of alcohol, this solution being filtered, and then there is added to it one-third of its weight of sodium carbonate. Apply this mixture with a brush, and repeat the coats at intervals until the surface has the appearance of polished mahogany. In case the luster should fail it may be restored by rubbing with a little raw linseed oil. The description of the process is meager, and hence he who would try it will have to experiment a little.

A good cheap mission effect for oak is to mix together equal parts of boiled linseed oil and good asphaltum varnish, and apply this to the wood with a brush; in a minute or so you may rub off surplus with a rag, and when dry give a coat of varnish. A gallon of this stain will cover about 600 sq. ft.

FILLING OAK

A very good hardwood filler for oak, either for a natural or golden effect, may be made from two parts of turpentine and one part of raw linseed oil, with a small amount of good japan to dry in the usual time. To this liquid add bolted gilder's whiting to form a suitable paste, it may be made thin enough for use, if to be used at once, or into a stiff paste for future use, when it can be thinned down for use, says Woodworkers' Review. After applying a coat of filler, let stand until it turns gray, which requires about 20 minutes, depending upon the amount of japan in the filler, when it should be rubbed off with cotton waste or whatever you use for the purpose. A filler must be rubbed well into the wood, the surplus only being removed. The application of a coat of burnt umber stain to the wood before filling is in order, which will darken the wood to the proper depth if you rub off the surplus, showing the grain and giving a golden oak effect. The filling should stand at least a day and night before applying shellac and varnish.

WAX FINISHING

In wax-finishing hardwoods, use a paste filler and shellac varnish to get a good surface. Of course, the wax may also be rubbed into the unfilled wood but that gives you quite a different effect from the regular wax polish, says a correspondent of Wood Craft. With soft woods you first apply a stain, then apply a liquid filler or shellac, according to the quality of work to be done. The former for the cheaper job. The usual proportion of wax and turpentine is two parts of the former to one part of the latter, melting the wax first, then adding the spirits of turpentine. For reviving or polishing furniture you can add three or four times as much turpentine as wax, all these proportions to be by weight. To produce the desired egg-shell gloss, rub vigorously with a brush of stiff bristles or woolen rag.

THE FUMING OF OAK

Darkened oak always has a better appearance when fumed with ammonia. This process is rather a difficult one, as it requires an airtight case, but the description herewith given may be entered into with as large a case as the builder cares to construct.

Oak articles can be treated in a case made from a tin biscuit box, or any other metal receptacle of good proportions, provided it is airtight. The oak to be fumed is arranged in the box so the fumes will entirely surround the piece; the article may be propped up with small sticks, or suspended by a string. The chief point is to see that no part of the wood is covered up and that all surfaces are exposed to the fumes. A saucer of ammonia is placed in the bottom of the box, the lid or cover closed, and all joints sealed up by pasting heavy brown paper over them. Any leakage will be detected if the nose is placed near the tin and farther application of the paper will stop the holes. A hole may be cut in the cover and a piece of glass fitted in, taking care to have all the edges closed. The process may be watched through the glass and the article removed when the oak is fumed to the desired shade. Wood stained in this manner should not be French polished or varnished, but waxed.

The process of waxing is simple: Cut some beeswax into fine shreds and place them in a small pot or jar. Pour in a little turpentine, and set aside for half a day, giving it an occasional stir. The wax must be thoroughly dissolved and then more turpentine added until the preparation has the consistency of a thick cream. This can be applied to the wood with a rag and afterward brushed up with a stiff brush.

HOW TO MAKE BLACK WAX

When putting a wax finish on oak or any open-grained wood, the wax will often show white streaks in the pores of the wood. These streaks cannot be removed by rubbing or brushing. Prepared black wax can be purchased, but if you do not have any on hand, ordinary floor wax can be colored black. Melt the floor wax in a can placed in a bucket of hot water. When the wax has become liquid mix thoroughly into it a little drop black or lampblack. Allow the wax to cool and harden. This wax will not streak, but will give a smooth, glossy finish.

THE 40 STYLES OF CHAIRS

There are 40 distinct styles of chairs embracing the period from 3000 B. C. to 1900 A. D.—nearly 7,000 years. Of all the millions of chairs made during the centuries, each one can be classified under one or more of the 40 general styles shown in the chart. This chart was compiled by the editor of Decorative Furniture. The Colonial does not appear on the chart because it classifies under the Jacobean and other styles. A condensed key to the chart follows:

Egyptian.—3000 B. C. to 500 B. C. Seems to have been derived largely from the Early Asian. It influenced Assyrian and Greek decorations, and was used as a motif in some French Empire decoration. Not used in its entirety except for lodge rooms, etc.

Grecian.—700 B. C. to 200 B. C. Influenced by Egyptian and Assyrian styles. It had a progressive growth through the Doric, Ionic and Corinthian periods. It influenced the Roman style and the Pompeian, and all the Renaissance styles, and all styles following the Renaissance, and is still the most important factor in decorations today.

Roman.—750 B. C. to 450 A. D. Rome took her art entirely from Greece, and the Roman is purely a Greek development. The Roman style "revived" in the Renaissance, and in this way is still a prominent factor in modern decoration.

Pompeian.—100 B. C. to 79 A. D. Sometimes called the Grecian-Roman style, which well describes its components. The style we know as Greek was the Greek as used in public structures. The Pompeian is our best idea of Greek domestic decoration. Pompeii was long buried, but when rediscovered it promptly influenced all European styles, including Louis XVI, and the various Georgian styles.

Byzantine.—300 A. D. to 1450 A. D. The "Eastern Roman" style, originating in the removal of the capital of the Roman Empire to Constantinople (then called Byzantium). It is a combination of Persian and Roman. It influenced the various Moorish, Sacracenic and other Mohammedan styles.

Gothic.—1100 to 1550. It had nothing to do with the Goths, but was a local European outgrowth of the Romanesque. It spread all over Europe, and reached its climax of development about 1550. It was on the Gothic construction that the Northern European and English Renaissance styles were grafted to form such styles as the Elizabethan, etc.

EGYPTIAN	GRECIAN.	ROMAN.
POMPEIAN.	BYZANTINE.	GOTHIC.
MOORISH.	INDIAN.	CHINESE.
JAPANESE.	ITALIAN GOTHIC.	TUDOR.

Moorish.—700 to 1600. The various Mohammedan styles can all be traced to the ancient Persian through the Byzantine. The Moorish or Moresque was the form taken by the Mohammedans in Spain.

Indian.—2000 B. C. to 1906 A. D. The East Indian style is almost composite, as expected of one with a growth of nearly 4,000 years. It has been influenced repeatedly by outside forces and various religious invasions, and has, in turn, influenced other far Eastern styles.

Chinese.—3500 B. C. to 1906 A. D. Another of the ancient styles. It had a continuous growth up to 230 B. C., since when it has not changed much. It has influenced Western styles, as in the Chippendale, Queen Anne, etc.

Japanese.—1200 B. C. to 1906 A. D. A style probably springing originally from China, but now absolutely distinct. It has influenced recent art in Europe and America, especially the "New Art" styles.

Italian Gothic.—1100 to 1500. The Italian Gothic differs from the European and English Gothic in clinging more closely to the Romanesque-Byzantine originals.

Tudor.—1485 to 1558. The earliest entry of the Renaissance into England. An application of Renaissance to the Gothic foundations. Its growth was into the Elizabethan.

Italian Renaissance, Fifteenth Century.—1400 to 1500. The birth century of the Renaissance. A seeking for revival of the old Roman and Greek decorative and constructive forms.

Italian Renaissance, Sixteenth Century.—1500 to 1600. A period of greater elaboration of detail and more freedom from actual Greek and Roman models.

Italian Renaissance, Seventeenth Century.—1600 to 1700. The period of great elaboration and beginning of reckless ornamentation.

Spanish Renaissance.—1500 to 1700. A variation of the Renaissance spirit aused by the combination of three distinct styles—the Renaissance as known in Italy, the Gothic and the Moorish. In furniture the Spanish Renaissance is almost identical with the Flemish, which it influenced.

Dutch Renaissance.—1500 to 1700. A style influenced alternately by the French and the Spanish. This style and the Flemish had a strong influence on the English William and Mary and Queen Anne styles, and especially on the Jacobean.

German Renaissance.—1550 to 1700. A style introduced by Germans who had gone to Italy to study. It was a heavy treatment of the Renaissance spirit, and merged into the German Baroque about 1700.

Francis I.—1515 to 1549. The introductory period when the Italian Renaissance found foothold in France. It is almost purely Italian, and was the forerunner of the Henri II.

Henri II.—1549 to 1610. In this the French Renaissance became differentiated from the Italian, assuming traits that were specifically French and that were emphasized in the next period.

Louis XIII.—1616 to 1643. A typically French style, in which but few traces of its derivation from the Italian remained. It was followed by the Louis XIV.

Elizabethan.—1558 to 1603. A compound style containing traces of the Gothic, much of the Tudor, some Dutch, Flemish and a little Italian. Especially noted for its fine wood carving.

Jacobean.—1603 to 1689. The English period immediately following the Elizabethan, and in most respects quite similar. The Dutch influence was, however, more prominent. The Cromwellian, which is included in this period, was identical with it.

William and Mary.—1689 to 1702. More Dutch influences. All furniture lighter and better suited to domestic purposes.

RENAISSANCE
ITALIAN 15th Century

Chair back.   Seat

RENAISSANCE
ITALIAN 16th Century

ITAL. REN. 17th Cent'y

SPANISH RENAIS'CE

DUTCH RENAIS CE.

GERMAN RENAIS'CE

FRANCOIS

HENRI II.

LOUIS XIII.

ELIZABETHAN.

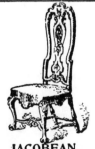

JACOBEAN.

WILLIAM & MARY

Queen Anne.—1702 to 1714. Increasing Dutch influences. Jacobean influence finally discarded. Chinese influence largely present.

Louis XIV.—1643 to 1715. The greatest French style. An entirely French creation, marked by elegance and dignity. Toward the end of the period it softened into the early Rococo.

Georgian.—1714 to 1820. A direct outgrowth of the Queen Anne, tempered by the prevailing French styles. It includes Chippendale, Hepplewhite and Sheraton, but these three great cabinetmakers were sufficiently distinct from the average Georgian to be worthy separate classification.

Chipppendale.—1754 to 1800. The greatest English cabinet style. Based on the Queen Anne, but drawing largely from the Rococo, Chinese and Gothic, he produced three distinct types, viz.: French Chippendale, Chinese Chippendale and Gothic Chippendale. The last is a negligible quantity.

Louis XV.—1715 to 1774. The Rococo period. The result of the efforts of .French designers to enliven the Louis XIV, and to evolve a new style out of one that had reached its logical climax.

Hepplewhite.—1775 to 1800. Succeeded Chippendale as the popular English cabinetmaker. By many he is considered his superior. His work is notable for a charming delicacy of line and design.

Louis XVI.—1774 to 1793. The French style based on a revival of Greek forms, and influenced by the discovery of the ruins of Pompeii.

Sheraton.—1775 to 1800. A fellow cabinetmaker, working at same time as Hepplewhite. One of the Colonial styles (Georgian).

R. & J. Adam.—1762 to 1800. Fathers of an English classic revival. Much like the French Louis XVI and Empire styles in many respects.

Empire.—1804 to 1814. The style created during the Empire of Napoleon I. Derived from classic Roman suggestions, with some Greek and Egyptian influences.

New Arts.—1900 to date. These are various worthy attempts by the designers of various nations to create a new style. Some of the results are good, and they are apt to be like the "little girl who had a little curl that hung in the middle of her forehead," in that "when they are good they are very, very good, but when they are bad they are horrid."

QUEEN ANNE.   LOUIS XIV   GEORGIAN.

CHIPPENDALE.   LOUIS XV.   HEPPLEWHITE.

LOUIS XVI.   SHERATON   R. & J. ADAM.

EMPIRE.   BRITISH NEW ART.   L'ART NOUVEAU

MODERN

MODERN AUSTRIAN   SCOTCH NEW ART   ARTS & CRAFTS

MISSION

HOW TO MAKE A PIANO BENCH

All the material used in the making of this piano bench is 1 in. thick, excepting the two rails, which are ⅞ in. thick. The bench can be made from any of the furniture woods, but the case may demand one made from mahogany. If so, this wood can be purchased from a piano factory. The following stock list of materials may be ordered from a mill, planed and sandpapered:

1 top, 1 by 16 by 36½ in.
2 ends, 1 by 14 by 18 in.
1 stretcher, 1 by 4 by 31½ in.
2 side rails, ⅞ by 4 by 29½ in.
2 keys, 1 by 1 by 3½ in.
6 cleats, 1 by 1 by 4 in.

The dimensions given, with the exception of the keys and cleats, are ½ in. longer than necessary for squaring up the ends.

The two rails are cut slanting from a point 1½

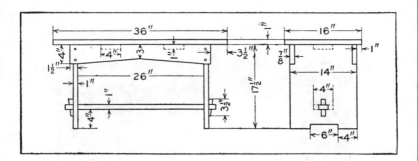

in. from each end to the center, making them only
3 in. wide in the middle.   The rails are "let into"
the edges of the ends so the outside of the rails and
end boards will be flush.   The joints are put together with glue and screws.   The cleats are fastened with screws to the inside of the rails and to
the top.   The stretcher has a tenon cut on each
end which fits into a mortise cut in each end. The
tenons will have sufficient length to cut the small
mortise for the key.

The kind of wood used will determine the color
of the stain for the finish.   This also depends on
matching other pieces of furniture.

HOW TO MAKE A MISSION SHAVING STAND

This attractive and useful piece of mission furniture will be appreciated by the person that does his own shaving. The shaving stand can be made at home by a handy man in his spare time as the stock can be ordered from a mill ready for making the joints and attaching the few pieces of hardware. The following is a stock list of materials:

    4 posts 1½ in. square by 50½ in.
    4 slats ⅞ by 1 by 32½ in.
    2 cross rails 1 by 1½ by 15 in.
    2 end rails 1 by 1½ by 13 in.
    1 top ⅞ by 16½ by 19½ in.
    1 bottom ⅞ by 15 by 17 in.
    2 ends ⅞ by 12½ in. square.
    1 back ⅞ by 12½ by 14½ in.
    1 door ⅞ by 6½ by 12½ in.
    2 drawer ends ⅞ by 6 by 7½ in.
    1 partition ⅞ by 12 by 14 in.
    1 partition ⅞ by 7 by 14 in.
    7 pieces of soft wood ½ by 7½ by 12 in.
    2 posts 1 in. square by 10½ in.
    1 bottom piece ⅞ by 1½ by 18½ in.
    4 mirror frame pieces ⅞ by 1½ by 14½ in.
    2 sticks for pins.
    2 hinges
    1 lock
    2 drawer pulls.
    1 beveled glass mirror 11½ by 11½ in.

While this piece of furniture can be made in any kind of wood, the novice will find that quarter-sawed oak will work up and finish better than the other woods. The stock list given has dimensions ½ in. larger in some instances for dressing and squaring where necessary.

The tenons and mortises are first cut for the cross-pieces at the bottom of the posts, and, as it is best to use dowels at the top, holes are bored in the bottom piece and also the ends of the slats for pins. The bottom piece is also fastened to the posts with

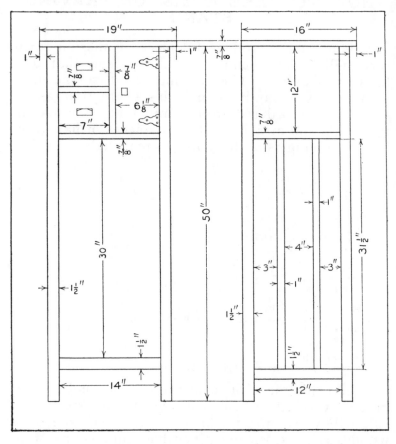

dowels. The bottom must have a square piece cut out from each corner almost the same size as the posts. When setting the sides together the end board and posts can be doweled and glued together

Shaving Stand Complete

and after drying well the posts can be spread apart far enough to insert the bottom rail and two slats. The rail and slats should be tried for a bit before putting on any glue, which may save some trouble.

After the sides are put together, the back is put in and glued. The top is then put on and fastened with cleats from the inside. The partitions are put in as shown and the door fitted. Two drawers are made from the ends and the soft wood material. The drawer ends may be supplied with wood pulls of the same material or matched with metal the same as used for the hinges.

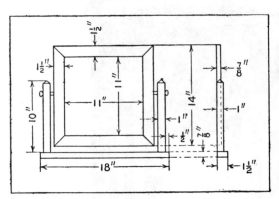

Mirror Frame and Standards Details

The pieces for the mirror frame must be rabbeted ½ in. deep to take the glass, and the ends joined together with a miter at each corner. The two short posts are tenoned and mortises cut in the bottom piece for joints and these joints well glued together. The bottom piece is then fastened to the top board of the stand. This will form the standards in which to swing the mirror and its frame. This is done with two pins inserted in holes bored through the standards and into the mirror frame.

After the parts are all put together, cleaned and sandpapered, the stand is ready for the finish.

A MISSION WASTE-PAPER BASKET

The basket shown in the accompanying sketch is designed to be used with a library table having

Waste-Paper Basket to Match Library Table

slats in the ends and wooden handles on the drawers. The finish is made to match that of the table by fuming, when completely assembled, in a large-

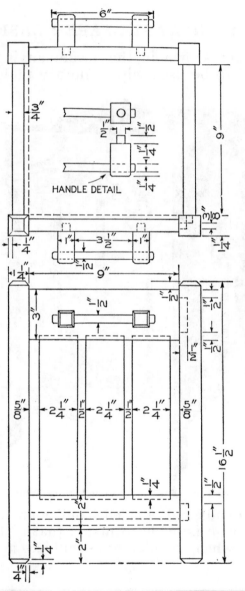

HANDLE DETAIL

Detail of Waste-Paper Basket

size, clean garbage can, with fumes of concentrated ammonia.

The following quarter-sawed white-oak stock should be procured in the exact dimensions given. This may be had, planed and cut to lengths, from a mill for a slight extra charge. It is advisable not to have them sandpapered, as the very coarse sandpaper generally used, gives a bad surface for finishing.

    4 posts, 1¼ by 1¼ by 16½ in., S-4-S.
    4 rails, ¾ by 3 by 10¼ in., S-2-S.
    4 rails, ¾ by 2 by 10¼ in., S-2-S.
    12 slats, ⅜ by 2¼ by 9½ in., S-2-S.
    4 handle pieces, 1 by 1 by 2½ in., S-4-S.
    2 handle pieces, ½ by ½ by 6 in., S-4-S.
    1 bottom, ⅜ by 9½ by 9½ in., S-2-S.

See that the posts are absolutely square cross section. Mark with a pencil—not gauge—the chamfers on the ends of the posts and plane them off.

Carefully mark the tenons on the ends of all the rails with a knife and gauge lines. Be sure that the distance from the tenon shoulder at one end of rail to the shoulder at the other end is exactly the same on each rail. Cut the tenons, using a backsaw and chisel.

Arrange the pieces as they are to stand in the finished basket, and number each tenon and mortise. Mark all the mortises on the posts, being sure to keep the distances between the top and lower rail the same on each post. Cut each mortise to fit the correspondingly numbered tenon. Next, mark the mortises for the slats in the rails, allowing the whole slat to go in ¼ in.

The handles are next in order. The pieces going into the rail should be fastened with a round

½-in. tenon cut on one end and glued in place. The crosspiece should be mortised all the way through these pieces and held in place by a brad from the under side.

Now put the whole basket together without gluing, in order that errors, if any, may be detected.

If everything fits perfectly, the basket is ready to be glued. For best results hot glue should be used. First glue up two opposite sides with the slats in place. Clamps must be used. When these have set for at least 24 hours, the other rails and slats may be glued in place and clamped. It is a good idea to pin the tenons in place with two 1-in. brads driven from the inside.

The handles are then glued in place, using hand screws to hold them until the glue sets. The bottom should rest on thin cleats, without being nailed to them, so that it may be removed when the basket is to be emptied of small papers, etc.

Before applying the stain, see that all glue spots are removed and all surfaces sanded to perfect smoothness. If a fumed finish is not desired, any good stain may be used, after which a thin coat of shellac and two coats of wax should be applied. Allow plenty of time for drying between the coats.

A CELLARETTE PEDESTAL

The illustration shows a unique article for the den. It serves as a pedestal and has one side which opens on hinges allowing the inside to be used as a smoker's cabinet or cellarette. All the lines are straight and the corners square, making it easy to

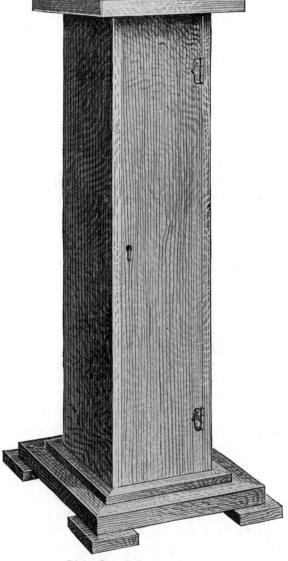

Plain-Oak Cellarette Pedestal

construct.　White oak will make up best, although ash, birch or southern pine may be used with good effect.

Stock of the following sizes should be bought, surfaced and cut to width and length:

2 top pieces, ⅞ by 12 by 12 in., S-2-S.
2 base pieces, ⅞ by 14 by 14 in., S-2-S.
2 sides, ⅞ by 8 by 35⅝ in., S-2-S.
1 back, ⅞ by 6¼ by 35⅝ in., S-2-S.
1 door, ⅞ by 6¼ by 34¾ in., S-2-S.
4 blocks, ⅞ by 4 by 4 in., S-2-S.
4 shelves, ⅞ by 6¼ by 6¼ in., S-2-S.
4 pieces, ⅞ by 1 by 10 in., S-4-S.

Make the top and base of two pieces, glued and screwed together with the grain crossed.　This method prevents warping.　To keep the end grain from showing, a strip of ⅜-in. lumber may be put on all around as shown in the drawing.

Have the sides, front and back squared up perfectly.　The sides are to overlap the back and to be fastened to it with round-head brass or blue screws. To the center of the top and base attach one of the 6¼-in. square pieces.　Over these, fit the sides and back and fasten them with screws or nails.　The four corner blocks are now put under the base.

Two or more shelves may be set in as shown. Brass or copper hinges will look well if a dark stain is to be used.

Around the sides and back a 1-in. strip should be fastened to the base to give added strength.

If a dull finish is desired, apply two coats of stain and two of prepared wax.　If a polished surface is wanted, first fill the pores of the wood with any standard filler, which can be purchased at a paint store.　After this has dried partly, rub off any surplus filler, rubbing across the grain of the wood.

When perfectly dry apply one coat of shellac and as many coats of varnish as desired, rubbing down

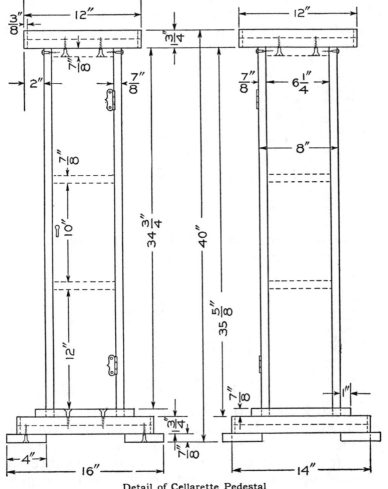

Detail of Cellarette Pedestal

each coat, except the last, with No. 00 sandpaper and pumice stone.

A DRESSER

The dresser shown in the illustration was made of quarter-sawed white oak and finished golden and waxed. The mirror is of beveled glass and the following is the stock bill:

1 top, ¾ by 19½ by 33 in., S-2-S.
4 posts, 1¾ by 1¾ by 28 in., S-4-S.
4 end rails, ¾ by 2¼ by 17 in., S-2-S.
4 stiles, ¾ by 2½ by 20 in., S-2-S.
2 panels, 3/16 by 12 by 18 in., S-2-S.
3 facings, ¾ by 2¼ by 29 in., S-2-S.
2 top frame pieces, ¾ by 2 by 32 in., S-2-S.
2 top frame pieces, ¾ by 2 by 19 in., S-2-S.
2 mirror supports, 1 by 2 by 33 in., S-2-S.
1 mirror support, ¾ by 2½ by 33 in., S-2-S.
1 drawer front, ¾ by 7¼ by 28 in., S-2-S.
1 drawer front, ¾ by 6¼ by 28 in., S-2-S.
2 drawer fronts, ¾ by 5¼ by 14 in., S-2-S.
1 partition, ¾ by 1 by 6 in.
2 mirror-frame pieces, ¾ by 2 by 40 in., S-2-S.
2 mirror-frame pieces, ¾ by 2 by 20 in., S-2-S.

The following material list may be of common stock and not quarter-sawed:

Mirror-backing pieces equivalent to ¼ by 18½ by 36 in., S-2-S.
2 cleats, ¾ by 2 by 10 in., S-4-S.
4 drawer-support frame pieces, ¾ by 2 by 29 in.
7 drawer-support frame pieces, ¾ by 2 by 15 in.
Slides taken from scrap stock, ¾ by 1 by 15 in.
3 back pieces, ¾ by 2¼ by 28 in., S-2-S.
2 back pieces, ¼ by 8 by 28 in., S-2-S.
8 drawer sides, ½ by 7¼ by 17 in., S-2-S.
2 drawer backs, ⅜ by 7 by 27 in., S-2-S.
2 drawer backs, ⅜ by 7 by 13 in., S-2-S.
2 drawer bottoms, ⅜ by 15 by 27 in., S-2-S.
2 drawer bottoms, ⅜ by 15 by 13 in., S-2-S.

In working up the various parts proceed in the usual manner. If not thoroughly familiar with the various tool processes involved, it will be necessary to investigate pieces of near-by furniture and to read up some good text dealing with the processes involved.

Dresser in Quarter-Sawed Oak

The exact size of the mirror is 18 by 36 in. and the frame should be rabbeted to correspond.

For a finish, a coat of paste filler colored so as to

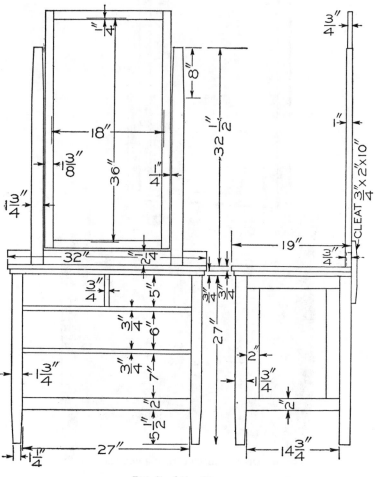

Detail of the Dresser

give a rich golden brown should be applied first. Allow this to harden, after rubbing and polishing it in the usual manner, then apply a thin coat of shellac. Sand this lightly when hard, and over this apply a coat of orange shellac. Over the shellac put several coats of some good rubbing wax and polish each coat well. If a striking contrast is wanted for the medullary rays of the quartering, apply a golden-oak stain first. Sand this lightly, then apply a second coat diluted one-half with solvent and sand again lightly. Apply a thin coat of shellac, then, when dry, sand lightly and apply paste, and proceed as before.

A MISSION SIDEBOARD

Oak is the most suitable material for making this sideboard and it should be first-class stock, planed and cut to the dimensions given in the following list:

1 top, ⅞ by 22 by 48 in., S-2-S.
1 top shelf, ⅞ by 12 by 48 in., S-2-S.
1 bottom, ⅞ by 22 by 48 in., S-2-S.
2 back posts, 2 by 2 by 57 in., S-4-S.
2 front posts, 2 by 2 by 36 in., S-4-S.
2 standards, 2 by 2 by 20 in., S-4-S.
2 mirror rails, ⅞ by 2 by 47 in., S-2-S.
2 mirror rails, ⅞ by 2 by 20 in., S-2-S.
3 front and back rails, ⅞ by 3 by 46 in., S-2-S.
4 end rails, ⅞ by 3 by 20 in., S-2-S.
4 standard rails, ⅞ by 2 by 10 in., S-2-S.
2 vertical pieces, ⅞ by 19½ by 22 in., S-2-S.
1 horizontal piece, ⅞ by 22 by 14¼ in., S-2-S.
1 drawer front, ⅞ by 6 by 14¼ in., S-2-S.
1 piece, ⅞ by 3 by 3 in.
4 vertical door pieces, ⅞ by 2 by 17 in., S-2-S.
4 horizontal door pieces, ⅞ by 2 by 15 in., S-2-S.
2 drawer sides, ⅞ by 5 by 14 in., S-2-S.
1 drawer bottom, ¼ by 14 by 14¼ in., S-2-S.
1 back panel, ¼ by 16½ by 44½ in., S-2-S.
2 door panels, ¼ by 10½ by 15½ in., S-2-S.
2 side panels, ¼ by 18½ by 16½ in., S-2-S.

Begin work by cutting the posts to the length indicated in the detail drawing. The top ends are

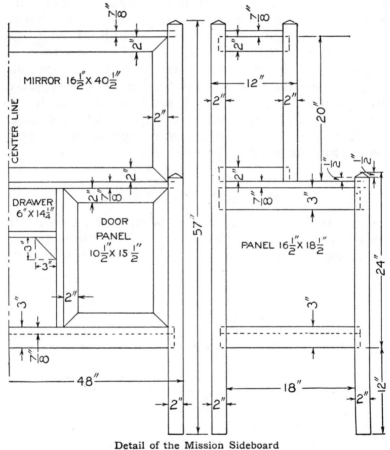

Detail of the Mission Sideboard

tapered with a ½-in. slant. These posts are cut in pairs and it is best to stand them up in the same

position they will be in the finished sideboard, and mark the sides to be mortised with a pencil. Also

Mission Sideboard in Quarter-Sawed Oak

cut the grooves into which the panels are to fit. These are to be ¼ in. wide and a little over ¼ in. deep.

The rails are cut with tenon ends to match the mortises, and also have grooves to receive the panels.

The bottom part of the back is closed with a panel and two rails, one at the same height from the floor as the front bottom rail, and the top one even with the under side of the top. The large panel is for the opening thus formed.

These parts are now put together, using plenty of good hot glue, and spreading it well on the mortises and tenon ends.

When drawing the frame together with the clamps, care must be taken to get it square.

After the glue is hard enough to remove the clamps, the top and bottom are put in place. The corners of the top are notched out to fit around the posts, while the bottom is cut to fit on the inside of the rails and is held in place by putting screws in at an angle through the bottom into the rails. The top is also fastened in this way, except that the screws are run through the rails into the top.

The two vertical pieces are now put in place. Drive nails through the bottom and into these pieces. On the top end use screws driven at an angle. Glue may be used if desired.

The doors are made to match these openings. The corners are mitered and the backs rabbeted to receive the panels. These panels may be made in art glass if so desired.

The horizontal piece for the drawer to rest upon is now put in place and fastened by driving nails through the vertical pieces. The drawer is made to fit this opening, and it should be lined with velvet to keep the silverware in good condition.

The standards and shelves are put on as shown in the drawing. The mirror is put in a frame, which is made to fit the back opening and has the corners mitered and the back rabbeted to receive the mirror.

Thoroughly scrape and sandpaper all parts that are visible. The sideboard is now ready to be finished as desired.

A HALL OR WINDOW SEAT

A simple design for a hall or window seat is shown in the accompanying sketch and detail drawing. Anyone who has a few sharp tools, and is at

Seat Made of Quarter-Sawed Oak

all handy with them, can make this useful and attractive piece of furniture in a few spare hours.

Quarter-sawed oak is the best wood to use in its construction, as it looks best when finished and is easy to procure. If the stock is ordered from the mill ready cut to length, squared and sanded, much of the labor will be saved. The following is a list of the material needed:

```
4 corner posts, 1½ by 1½ by 28 in., S-4-S.
2 side rails, ¾ by 2½ by 36½ in., S-4-S.
2 end rails, ¾ by 4 by 14½ in., S-4-S.
2 side braces, 1 by 1 by 36½ in., S-4-S.
2 end braces, 1 by 1 by 14½ in., S-4-S.
1 seat, 1 by 16 by 35¾ in., S-4-S.
2 top end braces, ¾ by 2 by 14½ in., S-4-S.
6 slats, ¾ by 2 by 6½ in., S-4-S.
```

Square up the four posts and lay out the mortises according to the drawing. To do this, lay them on a flat surface with the ends square and mark them with a try-square. The tenons on the end and side rails are laid out in the same manner as the posts. The end rails should be marked and mortises cut for the upright slats as shown in the detail drawing. Fit the end and side braces with mortise and tenon joints.

The two end frames can now be glued and clamped together and set away to dry. Put all the parts together before gluing to see that they fit square and tight.

The seat should be made of one piece if possible, otherwise two or more boards will have to be glued together. The corners should be cut out to fit around the posts. It rests on the side rails and cleats fastened to the inner side of the end rails.

When the window seat is complete go over it carefully and scrape all the surplus glue from about the joints, as the finish will not take where there is any glue. Remove all rough spots with fine sandpaper, then apply the stain best liked, which may be any one of the many mission stains supplied by

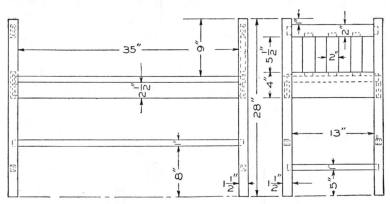

Detail of the Hall or Window Seat

the trade for this purpose. If this window seat is well made and finished, it will be an ornament to any home.

A MISSION PLANT STAND

For the mission plant stand shown in the illustration secure the following list of quarter-sawed white-oak stock, cut and finished to size:

1 top, ¾ by 15½ by 15½ in., S-2-S.
4 posts, 1¼ by 1¼ by 20 in., S-4-S.
4 rails, ¾ by 3 by 11 in., S-2-S.
2 rails, ¾ by 2 by 11 in., S-2-S.
1 shelf, ¾ by 6 by 10 in., S-2-S.
4 slats, ¼ by 2 by 12¼ in., S-2-S.
2 slats, ¼ by 2 by 12¾ in., S-2-S.

Test all surfaces of the posts with a try-square to see that they are square with each other. Lay out the tenons on the ends of the rails as shown in the sketch and cut with a tenon saw and chisel. Arrange the posts and rails as they are to stand and number each tenon and mortise. Lay out the mortises in the legs, taking the measurements directly from the tenon which is to fit that mortise. Cut the mortises, first having bored to the depth with a ¼-in. bit.

The slats should now be made and mortised into the top rail ¼ in. They come outside of the lower

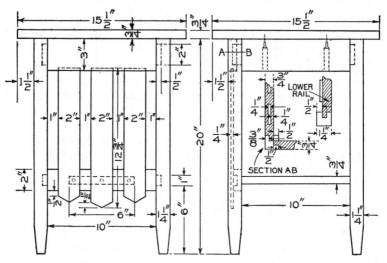

Detail of the Plant Stand

rail and are held to it with two small brads, fancy-headed tacks, or round-head screws.

In laying out the mortises for the lower rails, care must be taken to have them set ⅛ in. farther in than the upper rails so the slats may come outside.

Set up the stand without glue or screws to see that all pieces fit accurately. Then glue up the sides

with the slats first. After these have set for 24
hours, fit in the other two rails and the shelf. Three
flat-head screws should be used to hold the shelf
in place. These must be placed so the slats will
cover them when they are attached.

Complete Plant Stand

When this work is completed it is ready for the
top. A good method of attaching the top is shown
in the sketch. The screws used for fastening should
be 2-in. No. 10. Bore into the rail 1½ in. with a
bit $\frac{1}{16}$ in. larger than the head of the screw. Then
bore through the rest of the way with a bit a little

larger than the shank of the screw. Thus a little space is left for expansion and shrinkage of the top.

Scrape and sandpaper thoroughly to remove all marks or glue spots. Finish with two coats of weathered-oak stain, followed by two coats of black wax.

A BEDSIDE MEDICINE STAND

The accompanying sketch and detail drawing show a design of a bedside stand. This is a very desirable piece of furniture and is simple and easy to make. Quarter-sawed oak is the best wood to use in its construction. The material should be ordered from the mill ready cut to length, squared and sanded. The following list of material will be required:

```
4 posts, 1¾ by 1¾ by 33 in., S-4-S.
1 top board, 1 by 19 by 19 in., S-4-S.
3 intermediate boards, ¾ by 15½ by 17 in., S-4-S.
2 side boards, ¾ by 5 by 15½ in., S-4-S.
1 back board, ¾ by 4¼ by 14½ in., S-4-S.
4 side rails, ¾ by 2 by 16 in., S-4-S.
1 door, ¾ by 9 by 14½ in., S-4-S.
1 back board, ¾ by 10¼ by 14½ in., S-4-S.
2 panels, ⅜ by 9½ by 15 in., S-4-S.
6 slats, ¼ by 1 by 8¾ in., S-4-S.
1 drawer front, ¾ by 4¼ by 14½ in., S-4-S.
2 sides for drawer, ½ by 4¼ by 16 in., S-4-S.
1 back for drawer, ½ by 4¼ by 13½ in., soft wood.
1 bottom for drawer, ½ by 13½ by 15 in., soft wood.
```

Start work on the four posts by rounding the top corners and shaping the feet as shown. The four posts are identical and the mortises should be laid out on all four at once so as to get them all alike. These should be carefully cut with a sharp chisel. On the inner surface of each leg cut a groove to

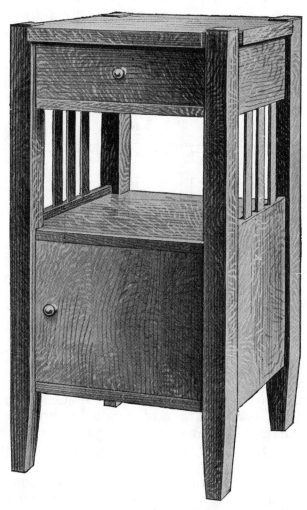

Medicine Stand in Quarter-Sawed Oak

hold the side boards of the lower compartment.
Next prepare the two wide and the four narrow
crosspieces, tenoning them to fit the mortises already cut in the legs. The lower crosspieces should
also have grooves cut in them to hold the side
boards of the compartment. The two complete
sides can now be glued and clamped together and

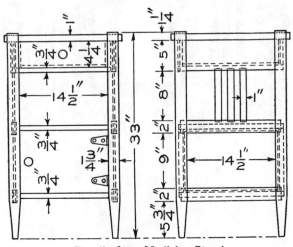

Detail of the Medicine Stand

set away to dry. While they are drying the remaining parts of the stand can be made. The three
horizontal boards are now made by notching out
the corners to fit around the legs. They are supported by fastening small cleats to the inner surface
of each crosspiece.

The two ends can now be set up and connected.
Notch out the corners of the top board and fit it in
place. The top is fastened down by means of screws
set in at an angle from below. The back boards can
be of soft wood and are fastened in place in the

usual manner. The door should be of one piece if possible and should have suitable hinges and a catch.

Make and fit the drawer in place, and the stand is ready for the finish. First scrape all the surplus glue from about the points so the stain will not be kept from the wood. Finish smooth with fine sandpaper, then apply stain of the color desired.

A MISSION HALL CHAIR

This hall chair is designed to take up as little room as possible. For its construction the following stock will be needed:

```
1 back, 7/8 by 14 by 44 in., S-2-S.
2 sides, 7/8 by 14 by 17 in., S-2-S.
1 seat, 7/8 by 14 by 14 in., S-2-S.
1 stretcher, 7/8 by 6 by 16 in., S-2-S.
1 brace, 7/8 by 5 by 11 in., S-2-S.
1 piece, 7/8 by 7/8 by 44 in., for cleats.
```

These dimensions are for finished pieces, therefore $\frac{1}{4}$ in. should be allowed for planing if the stock cannot be secured finished.

Lay out and cut the design on the back, sides, and brace. To cut the openings, first bore a hole near one corner to get the blade of a coping saw through and proceed to saw to the lines. Smooth the edges after sawing by taking a thin shaving with a sharp chisel. A file will not leave a good surface.

Mark the tenons on the ends of the stretcher and cut them with a backsaw and make smooth with a chisel. From the tenons mark the mortises in the sides through which they are to pass.

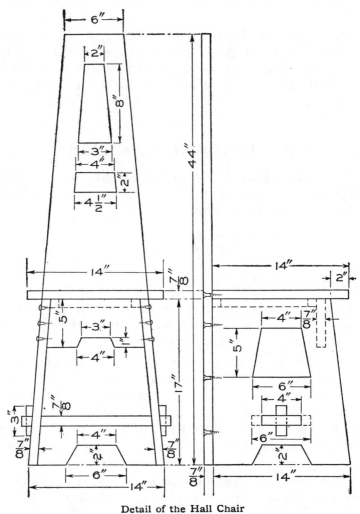

Detail of the Hall Chair

Complete Hall Chair in Plain Oak

To cut these mortises, first bore a row of holes with a ⅝ in. bit, boring halfway from each side so as not to split off any pieces. Now make of scrap material the two keys and from them mark the small mortises in the tenons.

Before putting the chair together, the cleats for holding the seat should be fastened to the sides, back and brace. Use flat-head screws for this purpose. Then put the sides and stretcher together, and fasten the back to the sides with flat-head screws.

The brace should be put in next, using three round-head screws in each end. There only remains the top, which is held by screws through the cleats from the under side.

Stain with two coats of weathered or mission-oak stain, and then apply a thin coat of "under-lac" or shellac and two coats of wax.

CONTENTS

MISSION FURNITURE

HOW TO MAKE IT

PART TWO

———

POPULAR MECHANICS HANDBOOKS

———

CHICAGO
POPULAR MECHANICS COMPANY

THIS book is one of the series of handbooks on industrial subjects being published by the Popular Mechanics Co. Like the magazine, these books are "written so you can understand it," and are intended to furnish information on mechanical subjects at a price within the reach of all.

The texts and illustrations have been prepared expressly for this Handbook Series, by experts; are up-to-date, and have been revised by the editor of Popular Mechanics.

THE dimensions given in the stock list contained in the description of each piece of furniture illustrated in this book call for material millplaned, sanded and cut to length. If the workman desires to have a complete home-made article, allowance must be made in the dimensions for planing and squaring the pieces. S-4-S and S-2-S are abbreviations for surface four sides and surface two sides.

AN OAK BUFFET

The accompanying sketch and detail drawing show
a design of a buffet wherein refinement of outline

Finished Buffet

and harmony of details are conspicuously regarded.
Quarter-sawed oak is the most suitable wood for
this handsome piece of mission furniture. The
material should be ordered from the mill ready cut

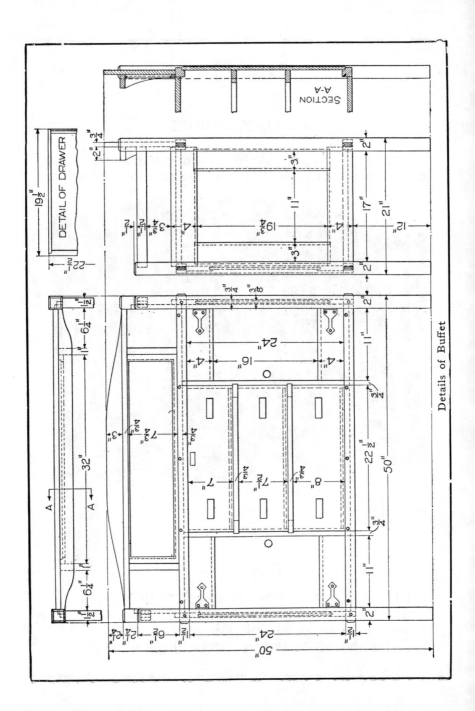

Details of Buffet

to length, squared and sanded. Following is a list
of the stock needed:

2 back posts, 2 by 2 by 47¾ in.
2 front posts, 2 by 2 by 45½ in.
4 rails, 1½ by 1½ by 50½ in.
2 end rails, 1½ by 1½ by 18½ in.
4 end rails, ¾ by 4 by 18½ in.
4 pieces for end panel, ¾ by 3½ by 21 in.
2 panels, ⅜ by 12 by 21 in.
1 top board, ¾ by 17½ by 47¼ in.
1 back board, ¾ by 11½ by 47¼ in.
1 shelf board, ¾ by 2 by 46 in.
2 brackets, 1 by 2 by 7¾ in.
4 pieces for doors, ¾ by 4 by 11 in.
2 panels, ⅜ by 11 bv 17½ in.
1 piece for drawer, ¾ by 8 by 22½ in.
1 piece for drawer, ¾ by 7½ by 22½ in.
1 piece for drawer, ¾ by 7 by 22½ in.
2 pieces, ½ by 8 by 19¼ in.; soft wood.
2 pieces, ½ by 7½ by 19¼ in.; soft wood.
2 pieces, ½ by 7 by 19¼ in.; soft wood.
1 piece, ½ by 8 by 19¼ in.; soft wood.
1 piece, ½ by 7½ by 19¼ in.; soft wood.
1 piece, ½ by 7 bv 19¼ in.; soft wood.
1 bottom board, ¾ by 17½ by 47¼ in.; soft wood.
2 partitions (several pieces), ¾ by 20 by 24¾ in.
2 front pieces, ¾ by 2 by 23 in.
2 back pieces, ¾ by 2 by 23 in.; soft wood.
2 side pieces, ¾ by 2 by 21½ in.; soft wood.
1 back (several pieces), ⅜ by 25 by 46 in.
1 mirror frame (to suit mirror).

Start to work on the four posts by squaring them
up to the proper length in pairs and beveling the tops
as shown. Clamp all four pieces on a flat surface
with the bottom ends even, then lay out the mortises
for the rails and panels on all four pieces at once
with a try-square. This insures getting the mortises
all the same height. The back posts also have a
mortise cut in them at the top for the back board as
shown. Lay out the tenons on the ends of the front
and back rails in the same manner. Cut them to fit
the mortises in the posts, also rabbet the back rails
for the backing. Cut tenons on the end rails and
rabbet them and the side pieces for the panels.

Lay out the top and bottom boards to the proper

size and notch the corners to fit about the posts. These boards are fastened to the 1½-in. square rails with dowels and glue. They can now be glued together and set away to dry. The top board is of oak, and be sure to get the best side up, while the bottom one can be made of soft wood if desired.

The partitions are made of several boards glued together. Be careful to get an oak board on the outer edge. The drawer slides are set into the partitions as shown and are fastened in place with screws from the inside.

The top back board has a tenon on each end that fits into the mortises in the back posts and is rounded at the top as shown. The shelf is also rounded at the ends and is fastened to the back with screws.

A plate glass mirror should be provided for the back. This is fitted to the back board as shown, then the brackets put up at the ends of the mirror frame.

The main parts are now ready to be assembled and glued together. Before applying any glue, see that all the joints fit together perfectly. The end rails and the panels are glued together first and allowed to dry. Be very careful to get the parts clamped together perfectly square and straight, else you will have trouble later on. When these ends are dry slip them on the tenons on the front and back rails which are already fastened to the top and bottom boards.

The back board and the partitions must be in place when this is done. Pin and glue the joints and clamp the whole together square and leave to dry.

The doors are now made by mortising the top and bottom pieces to take the ⅜-in. panel which is glued in place. The drawers are made as shown in the sketch. The front board should be oak, but the remainder can be made of soft wood. The joints are nailed and glued. Suitable hinges for the doors and handles for the drawers should be provided. Antique copper trimmings look very well with this style of furniture and can be secured at most any hardware store.

The back is made of soft wood and is put on in the usual manner. Scrape all surplus glue from about the joints, as stain will not take where there is any glue. Finish smooth with fine sandpaper, then apply the stain you like best. This can be any one of the many mission stains supplied by the trade for this purpose.

OAK STAIN

An easy and at the same time a good way to stain oak in imitation of the fumed effect, is to boil catechu in the proportion of ¼ lb. to 6 lb. of water, after which cool and strain. Apply this to the wood, and when dry treat with a solution of bichromate of potash in the same proportion as with the catechu. Bichromate of potash alone in water will give a good stain. A solution of 2 oz. of pearl ash and 2 oz. of potash mixed in a quart of water makes a good stain. Potash solution darkens the wood, and when applied very strong will produce an almost ebon hue, due to what we might describe as the burning of the wood fiber.

A PLAIN OAK HALL CLOCK

The hall clock shown in the illustration should be made of plain oak. The following pieces will be needed to make it:

2 back posts, 1½ by 1½ by 81 in., S-4-S.
2 front posts, 1½ by 1½ by 21 in., S-4-S.
2 front posts, 1½ by 1½ by 44 in., S-4-S.
10 front and back horizontals, 1½ by 1½ by 15 in., S-4-S.
10 side horizontals, 1½ by 1½ by 11 in., S-4-S.
1 face, ⅜ by 14 by 14 in., S-4-S.

FRONT DOORS

4 rails, ¾ by 1½ by 18 in., S-4-S.
4 stiles, ¾ by 1½ by 12 in., S-4-S.
4 horizontal mullions, 3/16 by ¾ by 11 in., S-4-S.
4 horizontal mullions, 3/16 by ⅝ by 11 in., S-4-S.
4 vertical mullions, 3/16 by ¾ by 15 in., S-4-S.
2 vertical mullions, 3/16 by ⅝ by 15 in., S-4-S.

BACK

1 piece, ⅜ by 14 by 21 in., S-4-S.
2 pieces, ⅜ by 14 by 18 in., S-4-S.
4 horizontal mullions, 3/16 by ⅝ by 14 in., S-4-S.
4 vertical mullions, 3/16 by ⅝ by 20 in., S-4-S.

TOP SIDE PANELS

2 pieces, ⅜ by 9½ by 14 in., S-4-S.
8 horizontal mullions, 3/16 by ⅝ by 9½ in., S-4-S.
6 vertical mullions, 3/16 by ⅝ by 14 in., S-4-S.
2 middle side panels, ¾ by 9½ by 20 in., S-2-S.

LOWER SIDE PANELS

8 vertical mullions, 3/16 by ¾ by 18 in., S-4-S.
8 vertical mullions, 3/16 by ⅝ by 18 in., S-4-S.
8 horizontal mullions, 3/16 by ¾ by 9½ in., S-4-S.
8 horizontal mullions, 3/16 by ⅝ by 9½ in., S-4-S.

If the worker will take the trouble to combine the different lengths of pieces having like thicknesses and widths into pieces of standard lengths, he will be able to save himself some expense at the mill with no more work for himself.

Begin work by shaping the ends of the posts as indicated in the drawing. Lay out and cut the mortises for the tenons of the horizontals or rails. These mortises need not be deep if the joints are to be reinforced later with lag screws as is the clock shown.

They may be what are known as stub tenons and mortises. The tenons are not more than ½ in. long, just enough to keep the rail from turning about.

Next lay out and cut the tenons on the rails. Bore the holes for the lag screws, being careful to bore on adjacent surfaces so that the holes will miss each other. Use a ⅜ by 3-in. lag screw, boring the hole in the tenon with a ¼-in. bit the full depth the screw is to enter.

The side panels should be fitted into grooves in the rails, and before the frame is put together these panels should be squared up and the grooves cut in the rails and posts at the proper places.

The mullions of the lower side panels, it will be noted, are specified ⅝ and ¾ in. wide. The ⅝-in. pieces are for the central parts of the frame and the others for the outside. The frame is to be made ⅛ in. larger all around than the distance between the posts and between the rails so that it may be set in

Hall Clock Complete

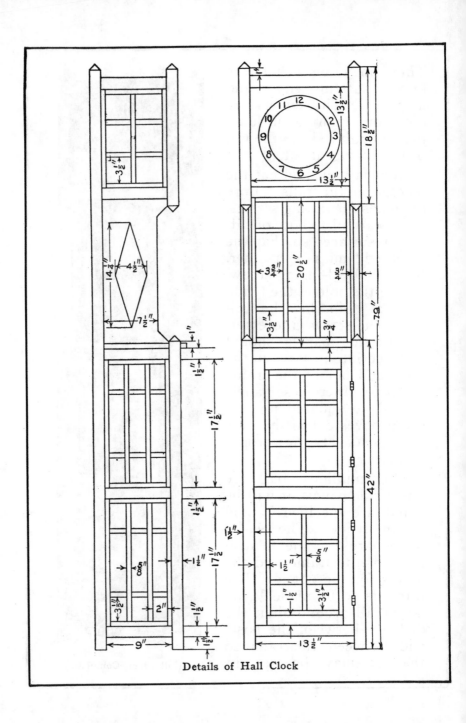

Details of Hall Clock

grooves cut in the posts and the rails to a similar depth, ⅛ in. This is true, also, of the mullions of the front doors. Square up the shelves so that they may be set into grooves in the adjacent rails. The middle shelf is to have an overhang and will rest upon the rails.

The mullions of the top side panels are all of the same width, and it is not intended or necessary to set their frame into grooves in the posts. The wood panel back of them gives ample strength.

It is a good plan not to groove the panel upon which the figures are placed, and which becomes the face of the clock. It is better to fit this piece in and fasten metal or wood buttons on the back side so that it can be readily taken off to get at the clock movement from the front.

Make the doors, tenoning the rails into the stiles and grooving both to receive the mullioned framework of $\frac{3}{16}$-in. stuff.

Put the whole frame together, using good hot glue for the joints. When the glue has dried sufficiently to allow the clamps to be taken off, fit the doors and hinge them. Butterfly surface hinges look well and are the easiest to apply.

Thoroughly scrape all the surplus glue off and sandpaper the parts preparatory to applying the finish.

To finish, apply one coat of mission oak water stain. When dry, sandpaper lightly, using No. 00 paper. Apply a second coat, diluted with an equal amount of water. Sand this lightly and put on a very thin coat of shellac to keep the filler color, which follows, from discoloring the high lights. When the shellac has had time to harden, sand lightly and put on a coat of paste filler. Use light filler, colored with umber and Venetian red in the proportion of 12 oz. of umber, and 4 oz. of red to 20 lb. of filler. The directions for applying the filler will be found on the can labels. On the hardened filler apply a thin coat of shellac. Sand the shellac lightly and put on several coats of some good floor wax, polishing well according to the directions on the can. This is what is known as a mission oak finish and is quite popular for this type of furniture design.

The metal figures for the dial come with the clock movement. Some of the movements come already set in boxes of wood so that all one needs to do is to shape the projecting ends of the wood containing boxes and fasten them to the frame with screws from the back. A clock with dial figures, eight-day movement, striking the hours and half hours, with cathedral gong can be bought for $4, possibly less.

A ROCKING CHAIR

In furniture construction such as this, nothing is gained by trying to plane up the stock out of the rough. This is mere drudgery and can be more cheaply and easily done at the planing mill by machinery. There will be plenty to do to cut and fit all the different parts. Order the pieces mill-planed and sandpapered to the sizes specified below.

Plain sawed red oak takes a mission finish nicely and is appropriate. Some people like quartered white oak better, however. The cost is about the same.

The stock for the chair is as follows: Widths and thicknesses are specified exact except for the rear posts and the rockers; but to the lengths enough sur-

Rocking Chair Complete

plus stock has been added to allow for squaring the ends.

2 front posts, 1⅝ by 2¼ by 22½ in., S-4-S.
2 back posts, 1⅝ by 11 by 40 in., S-2-S.
1 front horizontal, ¾ by 3½ by 22 in., S-4-S.
1 back horizontal, ¾ by 3½ by 20 in., S-4-S.
2 back horizontals, ¾ by 3½ by 20 in., S-4-S.
2 side horizontals, ¾ by 3½ by 20 in., S-4-S.
2 back slats, 5/16 by 3½ by 20 in., S-4-S.
2 arms, 1 by 4½ by 25 in., S-2-S.
1 rocker, 2¼ by 6 by 33 in., S-2-S.
5 bottom slats, ¾ by 2½ by 19½ in., S-4-S.

Begin work on the posts first. The front posts should have one end of each squared, after which

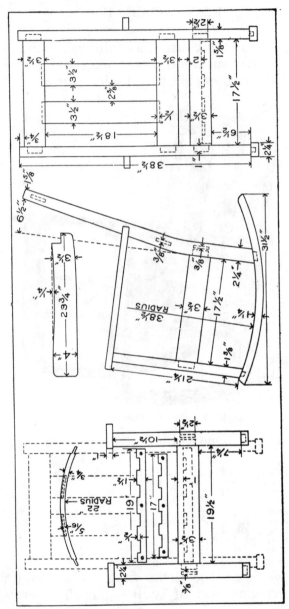

Details of Rocking Chair

they can be cut to the exact length. The rear posts, according to the stock bill, are specified for the exact thickness. By exercising forethought, both may be got from the piece ordered. The tops and bottoms of the posts should have their edges slightly chamfered to prevent their slivering.

The shape of the arm is a little out of the ordinary, but the drawing indicates quite clearly how it is cut. The arm is fastened to the posts by means of dowels and glue after the other parts of the chair have been put together.

Now prepare the curved parts of the back. These parts are worked to size, after which they are thoroughly steamed and bent in the forms described on another page. These forms should have a surface curve whose radius is 22 in. While the parts are drying out, go ahead with the cutting of the mortises and tenons of post and rail.

Inasmuch as the width of the front of the chair exceeds that of the back by 2 in., allowance must be made for slant either in the tenons of the side rails or in the mortises. This will necessitate the use of the bevel in laying off the shoulders of the tenons.

The slats for the bottom are made long enough so that their ends may be "let into" the front and back rails, a ¾-in. groove being plowed to receive them.

Assemble the back, then the front; and when the glue on them has dried, put the side rails in place, then the arms. The chair should now be scraped and sandpapered preparatory to applying the finish.

The cushion shown in the picture is made of Spanish roan skin leather and is filled with elastic felt. Such cushions can be purchased at the upholsterer's or they can be made by the craftsman himself. Frequently the two parts of the cushion are laced together by means of leather thongs.

———

A CURVED BACK ARM CHAIR

The arm chair, the picture and drawing of which is given herewith is a companion piece to the rocker described on another page.

With the exception of the back legs the stock bill which follows gives the thicknesses and widths exact. To the length, however, enough has been added to allow squaring up the ends.

Plain sawed white or red oak will be suitable for a design such as this.

Front posts, 2 pieces, 1⅝ by 2¼ by 26 in., S-4-S.
Back posts, 1 piece, 1⅝ by 8 by 45 in., S-2-S.
Front horizontals, 2 pieces, ¾ by 3½ by 21½ in., S-4-S.
Rear horizontals, 4 pieces, ¾ by 3½ by 19¼ in., S-4-S.
Side horizontals, 4 pieces, ¾ by 3½ by 19½ in., S-4-S.
Back slats, 2 pieces, 5/16 by 3½ by 19½ in., S-4-S.
Arms, 2 pieces, 1⅛ by 4 by 24 in., S-4-S.
Seat slats, 5 pieces, ½ by 2¼ by 20 in., S-4-S.

Begin work by squaring up the ends of the front posts and shaping the rear ones   Chamfer the ends of the tops and bottoms slightly so that they shall not splinter through usage. Next lay out the mortises and fenons.

The curved horizontals for the back should now be prepared and steamed as described on another page. The curved form to which the steamed piece is to be clamped to give shape to it should be curved slightly more than is wanted in the piece, as the piece when released will tend to straighten a little.

The arms of the chair may be shaped while these pieces are drying on the forms. The rails of the front and back may be tenoned, too. It should be noted that the front of the chair is wider than the back. This will necessitate care in mortising and tenoning the side rails so as to get good fits for the

Arm Chair Having Bent-Wood Back

shoulders   The bevel square will be needed in laying out the shoulders of the tenons.

Assemble the back, then the front. When the glue has hardened on these parts so that the clamps may be removed, put in the side rails or horizontals

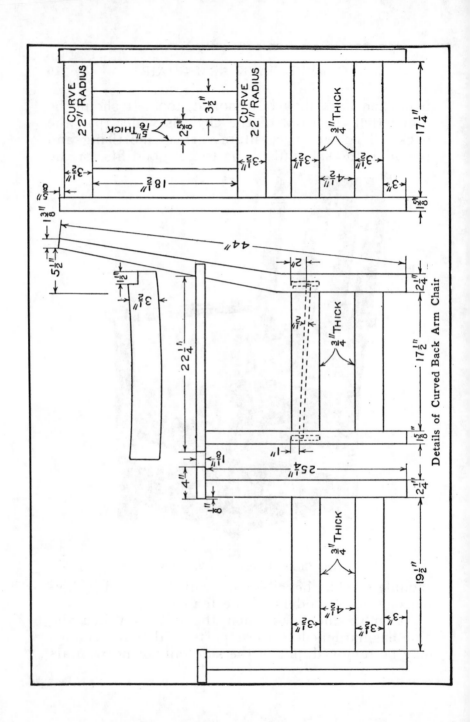

Details of Curved Back Arm Chair

and again adjust the clamps. The arms are to be fastened to the posts with dowels and glue.

The seat, it will be seen from the drawing, is to be a loose leather cushion to rest upon slats. These seat slats may be fastened to cleats which have been previously fastened to the inside of the front and back seat rails or they may be "let in" to these rails by grooving their inner surfaces before the rails have been put in place. The latter method is more workmanlike, but more difficult.

A cushion such as is shown can be purchased ready made up, or it may be made by the amateur by lacing together two pieces of Spanish leather cut to size and punched along the edges so as to allow a lacing of leather thong. It may be filled with hair or elastic felt such as upholsterers use.

Probably the simplest finish that can be used is weathered oak. Put on a coat of weather oak oil stain, sandpaper lightly when dry and then put on a very thin coat of shellac. Sand this lightly and follow with two or more coats of floor wax put on in very thin coatings and polished well.

A PLATE RACK

The plate rack shown in the accompanying illustration is designed for use in a room furnished in mission style. The dimensions may be changed to suit the wall space. The parts are held together entirely by keys. The bar across the front is for keeping the plates from falling out, but this may be left out if the plates are allowed to lean against the wall.

The following list of material will be needed, and,

if the builder does not care to do the rough work, the stock can be ordered planed, sanded and cut to the exact size of the dimensions given.

2 ends, ⅞ by 5 by 20 in.
1 top, ⅞ by 6 by 36 in.
1 shelf, ⅞ by 5 by 36 in.
1 bar, ⅞ in. square by 36 in.
4 keys. Scrap pieces will do.

Lay out and cut the mortises on the end pieces for the tenons of the shelf, also the tenons on the top

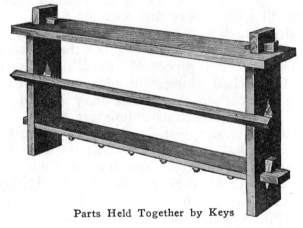

Parts Held Together by Keys

ends and the diamond shaped openings. In laying these out, work from the back edge of the pieces. Cut the tenons on the ends of the shelf to fit the mortises in the end pieces, numbering each one so the parts can be put together with the tenons in the proper mortises. Mark out and cut the mortises in the top to receive the tenons on the end pieces.

In laying out the mortises for the keys allow a little extra on the side toward the shoulder so the ends and tops may be drawn up tightly when the keys are

driven in the mortises. All the mortises and diamond shaped openings should be marked and cut
with a chisel from both sides of the board.

If the bar is used, it may be attached with a flat
side or edge out as shown.

Finish the pieces separately with any weathered
or fumed oak stain. When thoroughly dry, apply

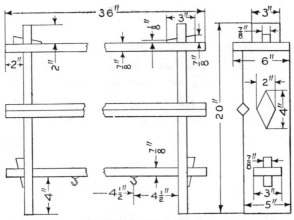

Details of Plate Rack

a very thin coat of shellac. Finish with two coats of
wax. The rack can be attached to the wall by two
mirror plates fastened on the back edges of the end
pieces.

TOOL FOR MARKING DOWEL HOLES

On some work it is quite difficult to locate the
exact point for a dowel, but with the tool illustrated
placed between the joint to be made and the parts
gently pressed together you have the exact point for
the dowel in each piece. The tool is made from a

piece of sheet steel about ½ in. square with a pin
having a point on both ends driven in the center,
as shown in Fig. 1. The tool is placed between the

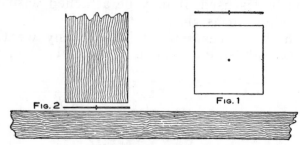

Marking Bore Holes for Dowels

pieces that are to be joined, as shown in Fig. 2.
The small pin will mark the point for the bit in both
pieces exactly opposite.

A MAGAZINE TABLE

This little magazine table will be found a very useful
piece of furniture for the den or library. Its small
size permits it to be set anywhere in a room without
being in the way. Quarter-sawed oak should be used
in its construction, and the following pieces will be
needed:

    4 legs, 2 by 2 by 29 in., S-4-S.
    4 end slats, ½ by 2 by 10 in., S-4-S.
    1 shelf, 1 by 16 by 30 in., S-1-S.
    1 top board, 1 by 18 by 36 in., S-1-S.

If you are convenient to a planing mill you can secure these pieces ready cut to length, squared and
sanded. This will save you considerable labor.

The four legs are finished on all sides and chamfered at the bottom to prevent the corners from split-

Table Complete

ting. The mortises for the shelf should be cut 9 in. from the top of each leg, as shown in the sketch. Care should be taken to make these a perfect fit.

The shelf should be finished on the top side and the four edges, and the corners cut out to fit the mortises in the table legs. An enlarged view of this joint is shown in the sketch.

The top board may have to be made of two 9-in. boards, dove-tailed and glued together. It should be finished on the top side and the edges. The edges can be beveled if desired. The board is fastened to the legs by means of screws through four small brass angles. These angles can be made or they can be purchased at any hardware store.

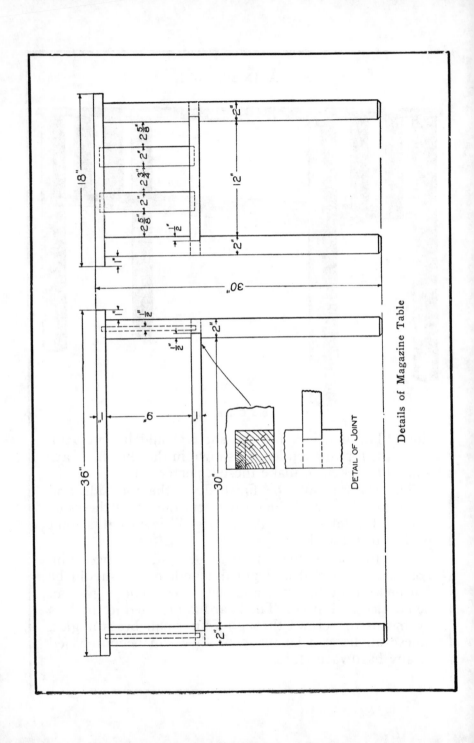

DETAIL OF JOINT

Details of Magazine Table

The top board and the shelf should be mortised at each end for the ½ by 2-in. slats. These slats should be finished on all sides.

The table is now ready to be assembled and glued together. The glue should dry at least 24 hours before the clamps are removed.

After the glue is dry, carefully go over the entire table with fine sandpaper and remove all surplus glue and rough spots. It can now be finished in any one of the mission stains which are supplied by the trade for this purpose.

A WASTE PAPER BASKET

A waste paper basket of pleasing design, and very easy to construct, is shown in the accompanying sketch. Quarter-sawed oak is the best wood to use, and it is also the easiest to obtain. The following pieces will be needed:

1 bottom piece, ¾ by 9 in. square.
4 corner pieces, ¾ in. square by 15½ in.
4 top rails, ¾ in. square by 7½ in.
12 slats, ¼ by ¾ by 16¼ in.
4 blocks, 1 in. square.
4 F.H. screws, 2½ in. long.
24 R.H. screws, ¾ in. long.

If the pieces are ordered from the mill cut to length, squared and sanded, much labor will be saved. First bevel the ends of the corner posts and the slats, as shown, and finish them with

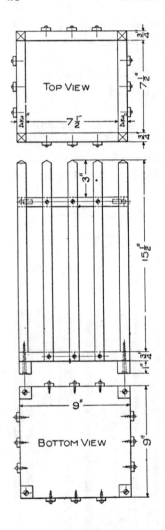

sandpaper. Bore the holes in the posts and the railing for the dowel pins. These pins should be about ⅜ in. in diameter and ¾ in. long. When this is done the parts can be glued together and laid aside to dry. The four blocks 1 in. square are for the feet. Bore holes through these blocks and the corners of the bottom board for the large screws to go through. Fasten them together by running the screws through the blocks, and the board into the ends of the corner posts as shown in the sketch. The ¼-in. slats can now be fastened on with the small round-headed screws. They should be evenly spaced on the four sides. This completes the basket except for the finish. This can be any one of the many finishes supplied by the trade for this purpose.

AN OAK WRITING DESK

For the writing desk shown in the accompanying picture the following stock will be needed. The thicknesses of all the pieces are specified. On the legs the widths, too, are specified. Quarter-sawed white oak is the best wood to use, and it should be well seasoned and clear of shakes and other imperfections.

STOCK BILL

2 front posts, 1⅝ by 1⅝ by 34 in., S-4-S., oak.
2 back posts, 1⅝ by 1⅝ by 42 in., S-4-S., oak.
2 lower side rails, ¾ by 3¼ by 15 in., S-2-S., oak.
1 lower back rail, ¾ by 3¼ by 27 in., S-2-S., oak.
2 sides, ¾ by 9 by 14 in., S-2-S., oak.
2 sides, ¾ by 10½ by 14 in., S-2-S., oak.
1 back, ¾ by 9 by 26 in., S-2-S., oak.
1 back, ¾ by 10½ by 26 in., S-2-S., oak.
1 top, ¾ by 6 by 30 in., S-2-S., oak.
1 lid, ¾ by 15 by 28 in., S-2-S., oak.
2 side shelves, ¾ by 5 by 16 in., S-2-S., oak.
4 braces, ¾ by 1¼ by 9 in., S-2-S., oak.
1 bottom of case, ¾ by 16 by 28 in., S-2-S., oak.

INTERIOR

1 piece, ¾ by 16 by 27 in., S-2-S., oak.
4 drawer and case bottom supports, ¾ by 2½ by 28 in., S-2-S., oak.
6 drawer and case bottom supports, ¾ by 2½ by 16 in., S-2-S., oak.
4 drawer guides, ¾ by ¾ by 16 in., S-2-S., oak.

DRAWERS

2 front pieces, ¾ by 7½ by 13 in., S-2-S., oak.
4 side pieces, ⅜ by 7½ by 16 in., S-2-S., poplar.
2 back pieces, ⅜ by 7 by 12 in., S-2-S., poplar.
2 bottom pieces, ⅜ by 16 by 12 in., S-2-S., poplar.

PIGEON HOLES

1 bottom, $\frac{3}{16}$ by 7¼ by 27 in., S-2-S., poplar.
1 top, $\frac{3}{16}$ by 4½ by 27 in., S-2-S., poplar.
4 verticals, $\frac{3}{16}$ by 7¼ by 10 in., S-2-S., poplar.
1 vertical, $\frac{3}{16}$ by 4½ by 4 in., S-2-S., poplar.
5 horizontals, $\frac{3}{16}$ by 7½ by 9 in., S-2-S., poplar.
2 horizontals, 4½ by 9 in., S-2-S., poplar.

DRAWERS IN PIGEON HOLES

2 front, ⅜ by 2¼ by 9 in., S-2-S., poplar.
4 sides, $\frac{3}{16}$ by 2¼ by 7¼ in., S-2-S., poplar.
2 backs, $\frac{3}{16}$ by 2¼ by 9 in., S-2-S., poplar.
2 bottoms, $\frac{3}{16}$ by 7¼ by 9 in., S-2-S., poplar.

Begin work by cutting the posts to length and shape. Having done this, lay out the tenons on the lower rails so as to have the required distances between the shoulders, and then cut them. Now cut the parts to

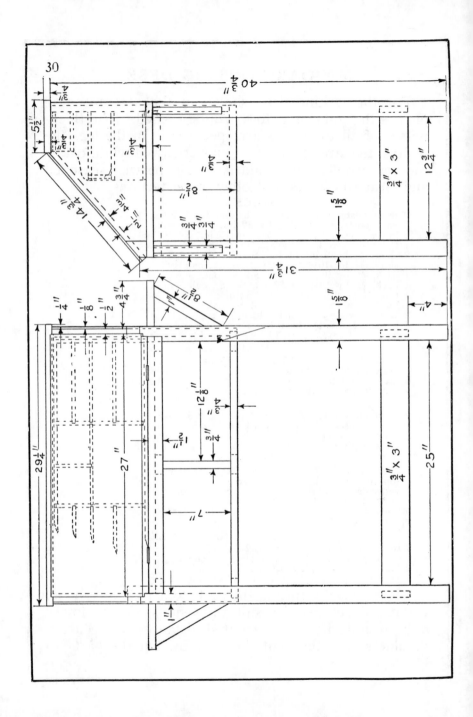

be worked into the frames that support the drawer and bottom of the case, and glue them properly. While this is drying, the other parts of the case may be laid out and shaped. It is intended that the sides of the case shall splice on the edge of the bottom

Writing Desk Complete

of the pigeon hole case. In this manner the side shelves will cover the joint on either end. The back may be made up into one solid piece. Make the side pieces of the case long enough to be housed into the posts about ⅜ in. at each end.

The shelves at the ends of the desk should be fastened after the frame is put together and before the bottom of the case for the pigeon holes is fitted and fastened. In so doing the shelves may be fastened from the inside of the case. The angles of the braces are 30-60 deg. It will be noted that the edges of the lid are rabbeted. Another way is to have the lid large enough to fit entirely over the sides of the case and change the slope to correspond.

The drawers may be made next. The fronts should be of oak, but the other parts of yellow poplar. An examination of an ordinary drawer will show the manner of construction.

Make the frame of the pigeon holes of $\frac{3}{16}$-in. yellow poplar. The drawing shows an arrangement entirely independent of the sides of the desk so that the frame can be made and slipped in place after the finish has been put on. Two drawers are shown. These are faced front and back alike so as to secure as much room in the drawer as possible.

In the finishing, the poplar wood should be finished with white shellac in the natural light color of the wood. For the oak parts the following is appropriate for this design: Apply one coat of green Flemish water stain. When this has dried, sandpaper lightly until the raised grain has been removed, and apply another coat of stain diluted one-half with water. When dry, sand lightly and apply a very thin coat of shellac. Sand lightly and apply a coat of dark filler, natural filler colored with lampblack, according to the somberness of the finish desired. Upon this put a coat of orange shellac. After this, put on two coats of a good rubbing varnish. Rub the first coats with curled hair or haircloth and the last with pulverized pumice stone and raw linseed oil or crude oil.

AN OAK COUCH WITH CUSHIONS

This beautiful piece of mission furniture can be made at a very moderate cost, if the material used for the cushions is of good imitation leather. These substitutes for leather last fully as long and the difference can only be detected by an expert. White oak will give the best results except for the frames or slats on which the cushions rest and these may be made of poplar or pine. If a mill or woodworking shop of any kind is handy, the hardest part of the work can be saved by securing the following list of material, cut, planed, sanded and squared up to the exact sizes given:

2 posts, 3 in. square by 17 in.
2 posts, 3 in. square by 26 in.
2 rails, ⅞ by 8 by 82 in.
1 rail, ⅞ by 8 by 25 in.
1 end, ⅞ by 18 by 25 in.
1 piece, ⅞ by 9 by 24½ in.

The last piece on the list when sawed diagonal makes the two slanting pieces at the head of the couch. The corner braces are made from two pieces of straight-grained oak, 2 by 4½ by 4½ in., sawed on the diagonal, and cut as shown in the enlarged plan section to make the four pieces.

First be sure the legs are perfectly square, the two short ones and the two long ones of equal length respectively. Either chamfer or round the upper ends as desired, chisel and plane the taper on the lower ends. Lay out and cut all the tenons on the rails—1 in. is the amount allowed at each end in the stock dimensions given. Arrange the posts and rails in the positions they are to occupy in the

Couch Complete

finished couch. Number each tenon and the place its corresponding mortise is to be cut in the post. Mark each mortise directly from the tenon which is to fit into it, taking care to have all the rails an equal distance from the floor. Bore and chisel out all mortises and see that all the rails fit perfectly, before proceeding with the work.

The next step will be to fit in the slanting side pieces at the head of the couch. These must be let into the long posts ½ in. and held also by a dowel in the side rail. In order to get these pieces into place, the mortise in the long post must be made ½ in. longer than the tenon on the sloping side piece so the tenon may be first pushed into the mortise and then the side clamped down on the rail over the dowel. The whole couch should fit together perfectly before gluing any of the parts.

Glue the end parts together first. Hot glue will hold best if the room and lumber are warm; if these cannot be had, use cold glue. After the ends have set for at least 24 hours, glue in place the side rails and slanting head pieces. Screw in place the corner braces. Be sure when making these braces to have the grain running diagonally across the corner, or the brace will be weak, also, be sure the sides are square with the ends; this may be determined by measuring the diagonals to find if they are equal.

If it is decided to use frames for the cushions, then the following material will be necessary:

    2 pieces, ⅞ by 2 by 56 in.
    2 pieces, ⅞ by 2 by 25 in.
    4 pieces ⅞ by 2 by 21 in.

This material may be of pine or poplar. These pieces are made into two frames as shown in the drawing and held together with long screws or nails. Fasten with glue and screw short blocks on the inside of the couch rails for holding the two frames in place. Tack pieces of cheap burlap across the frame and cover with ordinary black cambric. This will give a strong, springy rest for the cushions.

Should slats be used instead of frames for holding the cushions, then the following list of material should be substituted for the frame material list:

    2 cleats, ⅞ by 2 by 56 in.
    2 cleats, ⅞ by 2 by 25 in.
    12 slats, ¾ by 5 by 25 in.

The materials listed may be of soft wood the same as for the frame. The cleats are fastened to the in-

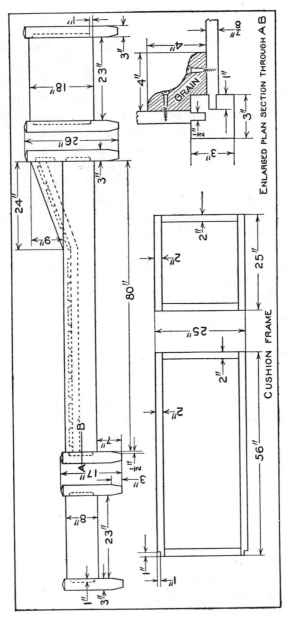

Details of Mission Couch

side of the rails of the couch with screws, so the top edge will be 2 in. lower than the top edge of the rails. The slats are spaced evenly on these cleats.

After the glue is all set, remove the clamps and scrape off any glue that may be on the wood. If this glue is not removed it will keep the stain from entering the wood, which will show up when finished in white spots.

This couch may be stained in any of the shades of brown or dark to harmonize with its lines of construction. A water stain will penetrate the wood best and after this is applied and thoroughly dried the surface should be well sanded to remove the roughness of the raised grain. Apply one coat of thin shellac and when this is dry, put on two coats of wax.

In making up the cushions, use either hair or elastic felt for the filling.

ELECTRIC SHADE FOR THE DINING ROOM

The dining shade shown is constructed of wood and glass. There will be needed the following:

8 pieces, ¾ bv ¾ by 24 in., S-4-S, oak.
4 pieces, ¾ by ¾ by 4 in., S-4-S, oak.
4 pieces, ¾ by ¾ by 10½ in., S-4-S, oak.
4 pieces, ⅜ by ¾ by 23 in., S-4-S, oak.
8 pieces, ⅜ by ¾ by 10 in., S-4-S, oak.
4 pieces, ⅜ by ¾ by 9 in., S-4-S, oak.
1 piece, ¾ by 8 by 8 in., S-4-S, oak.

Begin work by shaping the ends of the longest pieces as shown in the drawing. All the angles are 45 deg. Next lay out the cross-lap joints at the corners so that two sets of horizontal frames shall be formed 23 by 23 in. Cut four pieces to a length of 3 in. each. Also shape up the "false" extensions of these pieces which are to be fastened below the lower frame at the corners. Since these are to be cut from the pieces just specified, the easiest way is to shape the end of each to the required angle and then crosscut. Rabbet these pieces sufficient to al-

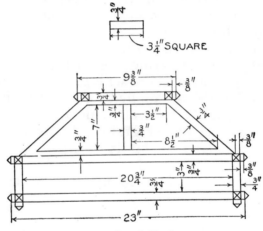

Details of Shade

low the art glass to set in on the back sides and be fastened—about ¼ in. will do—and put them together with glue and brads.

Now make the top square in a similar manner, except the rabbets. In this top square is to be fitted the ¾-in. board which is to hold the lights and to which the chains are to be fastened.

The sloping sides are next to be made. The sides are to be built up separately, the corners being lapped and glued after rabbeting the under arrises sufficient to let the glass in. The four sides are mitered together at their edges and reinforced by covering the joint with copper.

These sides are next mitered to the top and bottom frames and made fast on the under sides with copper strips, glue being used on the edges of the wood.

The shade shown had a mottled glass in which greens predominated. The sizes and shapes of these pieces of glass would better be determined after the woodwork is finished.

Electric Shade Complete

One manner of fastening the chains is clearly shown in the photograph. Such a combination will call for an extra piece of oak, ¾ by 3¼ by 3¼ in. finished stock.

A good finish for this shade is obtained as follows: Put on a coat of silver gray water stain.

When this has dried, sand lightly with No. 00 sand-paper and apply a coat of golden oak oil stain. Allow this to dry after wiping the surplus off with a cloth. Put on a coat of black paste filler and allow to harden over night. When dry, sand lightly and put on a coat of very thin shellac. Sand this lightly when hard and put on a coat of wax. This is a very dark finish relieved by high lights of lighter brown and is known as Antwerp oak.

HOW TO BEND WOOD

The process for making bent wood for furniture parts is the same as for any other kind of bent-wood work. The pieces should be made close to the size, with only enough material left on them for "cleaning up" after the bending has been done. The pieces used for the bent work should be good, clean, "live" lumber. Lumber dried on the stump will not bend.

A box must be made in which to steam the pieces of wood to be bent. A design of a steaming box is shown in the illustration. Such a box is made by nailing four boards together into a square or rectangular form, the boards having a length sufficient to take in the length of the furniture parts to be bent. Both ends of the finished box are squared up and closed with a board cut to the size, using felt or gunny sack in the joint to make it as tight as possible. These ends can be nailed on, but it is best to hold them with a bar of metal set against each one. Nailing the ends a few times would spoil the box for further use in steaming.

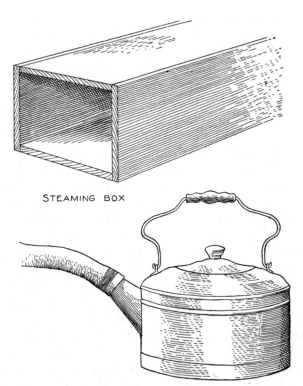

STEAMING BOX

HOSE ATTACHED TO TEAKETTLE

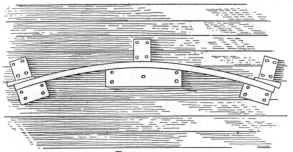

FORM BLOCKS

A good teakettle will serve the purpose for a steam generator. A hose is attached to the spout of the teakettle, as shown in the illustration, and to the steaming box in a like manner. The steaming box should be provided with a short piece of gas pipe turned into a hole bored into one of the sides used for the top on which to attach the hose. A small hole should be bored into one side of one end of the steaming box, and this end should be arranged a trifle lower than the other end. The hole will permit the water of condensation to escape. Steam should not escape from the box when a charge of wood is being softened. Steam which escapes from the box in the form of vapor has done no work whatever, and is just so much waste of fuel. In order to give up its heat to the wood, the steam must condense and come away from the box as water. Therefore, in steaming a charge of pieces in the box, never crowd the teakettle so hard that the steam escapes around the heads of the box or through any other joints. The steam should be supplied to the box just as fast as it condenses, and no faster. When the pieces are placed in the box they should be so arranged that the steam can find ready access to all sides of each piece.

The curve or bend of the piece to be made must be marked out on a wide board or on the floor. Nail down several blocks of wood or pieces cut out like brackets on the board or floor against the drawing, as shown in the illustration. The wood is sprung between these blocks or forms after it has been softened by steam. When taking the steamed pieces from the box do not lose any time in securing them to the forms. Do not take out more than one piece at a time, as it must be bent to the forms immediately after taking it from the hot steam. The time of the steaming will vary with the size of the pieces. Small strips may be steamed in 15 or 20 minutes, while large ones may require several hours to become soft enough to bend. The pieces must be left in the forms until they are thoroughly dry.

A SMOKING STAND

When making the smoking stand shown in the accompanying photograph, use quarter-sawed oak, if possible, as this wood is the most suitable for finishing in the different mission stains. This little piece of furniture is very attractive, easy to construct, and is an article that a smoker would appreciate.

If the stock is purchased finished and sandpapered, it will save much of the hard work. The material needed is as follows:

One piece, ⅞ by 12 in. by 9 ft. long, for the legs.
One piece, ⅞ by 10 in. by 4 ft. long, for the top.
One piece, ⅞ by 8 in. by 4 ft. long, for the shelves.
One piece, ½ by 2 in. by 6 ft. long, for the pipe rack.

The legs can be made first. Cut four pieces off the 12-in. board, each exactly 25 in. long, and lay each one out with a pair of compasses as shown in the detail drawing at Fig. 1. With a circle or keyhole saw cut out the piece, then shave out the saw marks and sandpaper smooth.

Next take the 8-in. board and make the shelves. Set a bevel protractor at a 45-deg. angle, lay out the pieces as shown in Fig. 5, and cut them out with a saw. Eight pieces are cut out as shown in Fig. 4. These pieces can be cut out of the scraps left from cutting the legs and shelves. Cut them so that the grain runs the long way. Place two of these braces on the bench with the beveled ends toward each other, but with a piece of $\frac{7}{8}$-in. stock between them, and the other two beveled ends resting against a straightedge. Fasten

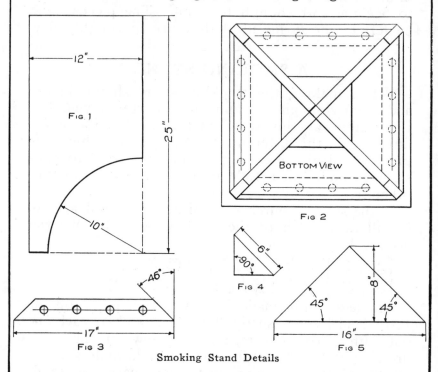

Smoking Stand Details

them to the bench with a couple of nails, leaving the heads sticking up so that you can pull them later with a claw hammer. Remove the straightedge and slide the piece that is between the braces along until it projects 4 or 5 in. from the side formed by the straightedge. Then place two more braces in the corners formed by this piece, put two 7/8-in. pieces between the two braces that are fastened, and the two that are loose, so that each brace will be in its proper place. Fasten the last two the same as the first pair. Then remove all the pieces from between the braces and

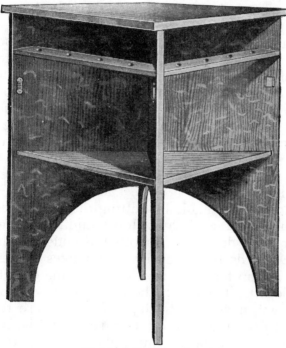

Finished Smoking Stand

place the tops of the legs in their stead. These should be fastened to the braces with 1-in. screws of small diameter, put in at an angle. Bore a hole in straight for about 1/4-in. with a 1/4-in. bit for each screw, and then run a gimlet at an angle into the leg. After you

have the legs fastened to the first set of braces, measure up from the bench 10 in. and put in another set,
being careful to get them all the same distance from
the bench, as the inner corners of the shelves rest on
these braces. Now pull out the nails and set the stand
on its feet.

Next put in the shelves. Place the inner corner of
one on one of the braces, and fasten it there with a
screw put through the brace from the bottom. Now
fasten a clamp on each leg at the ends of the shelf
in such a manner as to form a support on the top side
of the shelf. Then put four screws through the shelf
from the bottom into the legs. Repeat the operation
on each shelf, being careful to get them all the same
height. Four pieces like Fig. 3 should now be made.
These pieces will have to be fitted in place as they
should slant outward so that it will be easy to put
articles through the holes. The holes should be about
$5/8$-in. diameter.

The top can be made by cutting off two pieces from
the 10-in. board, each 20 in. long, and fastening them
together with dowels. Smooth the ends and be sure
that the boards match evenly. It makes a better job
to glue the top together, in addition to the dowels, and,
if you do this, it would be better to make the top first.
Then it will have time to dry before you are ready to
use it.   In putting on the top, care should be taken to
get each of the corners an equal distance from the
legs. Then a screw may be put up through each one
of the braces and two or three through each leg into
the top. Now smooth all rough and uneven places
with fine sandpaper and apply the finish. Secure
some metal matchsafes and scratchers, fasten on as
shown in the photograph, and the stand is complete.

A CHINA CLOSET

This beautiful piece of mission furniture can be made by anyone who has a few good tools and knows how to use them. The cost is very moderate and if you are convenient to a mill a great amount of labor can be saved by ordering the pieces ready cut to length, squared, and sanded. Quarter-sawed oak should be used and the material needed will be as follows:

4 posts, 2 by 2 by 54 in., S-4-S.
2 top and bottom boards, ¾ by 15¾ by 39½ in., S-1-S.
2 shelves, ¾ by 15½ by 38 in., S-2-S.
2 lower end braces, ¾ by 5 by 15 in., S-2-S.
2 upper end braces, ¾ by 4¼ by 15 in., S-2-S.
1 lower front board, ¾ by 3 by 40 in., S-1-S.
1 upper front board, ¾ by 2¼ by 40 in., S-1-S.
4 door frames, ¾ by 1¾ by 43½ in., S-2-S.
4 door frames, ¾ by 2 by 19 in., S-2-S.
4 upright end pieces, ¾ by 1½ by 39½ in., S-2-S.
5 back pieces, ½ by 8 by 46½ in., S-1-S.
2 cleats, 1 by 1 by 37¾ in., soft wood.
4 cleats, 1 by 1 by 12¾ in., soft wood.
4 blocks, ½ by 1 by 1½ in.

First be sure the posts are perfectly square and of equal length. Either chamfer or round the upper ends as desired. The mortises can be laid out and cut, or they can be left until the tenons are all made and then marked and cut directly from each tenon.

The top and bottom boards should have the corners cut to clear the posts as shown in the drawing. The top board should be finished on both sides and the bottom one on the upper side only and be sure to get the best side up.

Cut the tenons on the front boards back ¼ in. from the face as shown in the end view. The boards should be finished on the outside sides and edges. The end pieces are fitted and finished in a similar manner except that the inside edge is rabbeted for

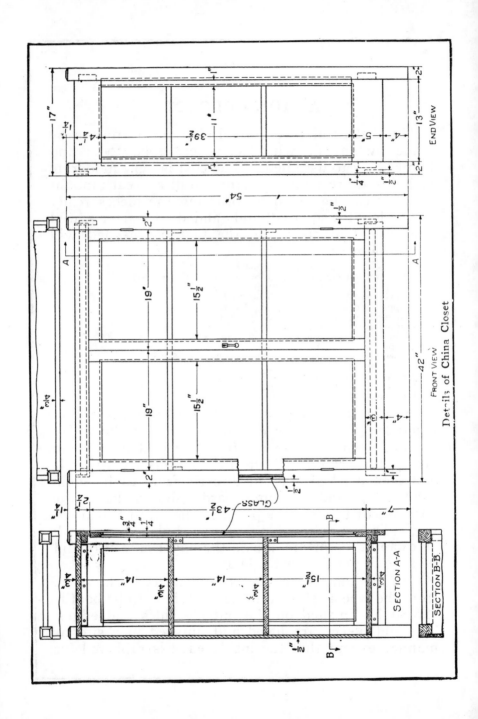

END VIEW

FRONT VIEW

Details of China Closet

SECTION A-A

SECTION B-B

the glass as shown. The side pieces are also rabbeted for the glass and the posts have grooves ½ in.
deep cut in them to hold these side pieces. They
are glued in place and this can be done after the
frame is put together.

China Closet Complete

The two shelves are finished on both sides and the
front edges. The doors are fitted in the usual manner by a tenon and mortise joint at the ends. They
are rabbeted on the inside for the glass and are
finished on all sides.

Before gluing any of the parts together, see that they all fit and go together perfectly square. The posts, side, and front pieces should be glued and assembled, then the top and bottom boards put in place to hold the frame square when the clamps are put on. Leave dry for about 24 hours, then scrape all the surplus glue from about the joints as the finish will not take when there is any glue. Fasten the top and bottom boards to the frame by means of screws through cleats as shown in the drawing. The backing is put on and finished on the front side. A mirror can be put in the back without much trouble, if it is desired. The shelves should be put in place and held at the back by screws through the backing and at the front by two small blocks on the posts as shown.

After the closet is all assembled it should be thoroughly gone over with fine sandpaper before any finish is applied. It can be finished in any one of the many mission stains which are supplied by the trade for this purpose.

A LEATHER-COVERED FOOTSTOOL

The illustration shows a very handy footstool in mission style. The following list of materials will be needed:

4 oak posts, 1½ by 1½ by 12 in., S-4-S.
2 sides, ¾ by 3 by 12 in., soft wood.
2 ends, ¾ by 3 by 8 in., soft wood.
1 bottom, ¾ by 8 by 12 in., soft wood.
1 small box of 8 oz. tacks
2½ doz. ornamental head nails.
1 piece of dark leather, 16 by 20 in.
½ lb. hair and a small portion of mission stain.

The posts are the only parts made of quarter-sawed oak, the other parts, being covered with leather, can be made of any kind of soft wood. Chamfer the top end of each post, and taper the lower ends as shown in detail. When this is done the mortises can be cut for the sides as shown in the post detail. When cutting the mortises and tenons take care to make them fit perfectly, as there is nothing to brace the legs at the bottom. The strength

Footstool Leather Covered

of the stool depends upon the joints. Make the surface of the posts smooth by first using No. 1 sandpaper, then finishing with No. 00.

The parts are now assembled. First clamp the ends together, using plenty of glue on the joints, and drive some small nails on the inside of the posts through the tenon ends. When the glue has set, the remaining sides can be put together the same as the ends. Fit the bottom on the inside about 1 in. from the top. This can be made fast by driving nails through the sides and ends of the board. The finishing is done by putting on the mission stain as the directions state on the can, then wax the surface to get a dull gloss.

The leather is now put on. Notch out the corners

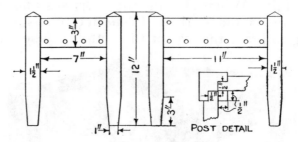

Details of Footstool

to fit around the posts, but do not cut the ends off. Lap them under the cover. Before nailing on the cover fix the hair evenly over the top, about 6 in. deep. Draw the leather over the hair and fasten the edges with the 8-oz. tacks. The ornamental nails are driven in last, as shown in the drawing, to make a good appearance.

ARTS-CRAFTS MANTEL CLOCK

The clock shown in the illustration was designed especially for rooms furnished in mission style. The clock, however, may be made of mahogany or other wood to match the furniture in any room where it is to be placed. If the mission effect is desired, an oxidized or copper sash should be used. Movements can be bought at the salesroom of a clock company. A movement should be selected that is wide enough from the front to the back to allow the clock case to be made sufficiently deep for standing without being easily upset.

Quarter-sawed white oak is the best material for this clock, but any other wood which works easily and takes a stain well may be used. Two pieces, ⅜ in. thick, 6½ in. wide, and 8½ in. long, will be needed for the front and back. One piece, 5 in. wide,

Mantel Clock with Wood and Copper Front

6 in. long, and with a thickness sufficient for the clock movement, is needed for the middle part. The thickness of this piece depends on the movement secured.

After the front and back pieces are finished, and a piece of hammered copper screwed on the front as shown in the drawing, the middle piece must be made just thick enough to make the whole distance from the front of the copper to the back of the clock equal to the depth of the movement. Plane one edge on both front and back pieces. Lay out the design and the centers for the circular holes from this planed edge. Use a plane and chisel to cut the outside design. The hole can be bored out with an expansive bit, or sawed out with a scroll saw, and filed perfectly round with a half-round wood file. The bit will give the best results. If the bit is used, bore holes in a piece of scrap wood until the exact size is found.

The outside design of the piece of copper is made to correspond to the design of the clock. The circular hole in the copper can be cut with the expan-

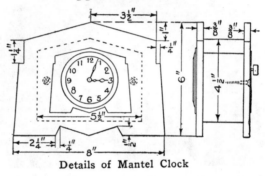

Details of Mantel Clock

sive bit by first punching a hole in the center to receive the spur of the bit, placing on a block of wood and boring through a little way. The spur on the cutter will cut out the copper. Fasten the copper to the front with copper nails or round-headed screws.

If good glue can be had, the three pieces of wood may be glued together. If the glue cannot be relied upon, put in two flat-headed screws from the back.

The clock can be finished with a dark stain and waxed, or, as it is small, it can be easily fumed. If stain is used, stain and wax the pieces before putting them together. The fuming process is more easily done after the clock is assembled. Secure a bucket, a peck measure, or any receptacle large enough, when inverted, to put over the clock. Pour about 2 oz. of strong ammonia into a saucer or small pan. Support the clock above the saucer and cover both with the inverted bucket. Allow it to stand for three or four days—the longer it stands the darker the fumed finish will be. Finish with two coats of bleached wax. Do not use ordinary uncolored wax, as it will show in the unfilled pores of the wood. The works of the clock should not be in the frame while fuming.

A MUSIC STAND

The attractive and useful piece of mission furniture shown in the accompanying illustration is made of quarter-sawed oak. Considerable labor can be saved in its construction if the stock is ordered from the mill ready cut to length, squared and sanded. The stock list consists of the following pieces:

    1 top, ¾ by 16 by 20 in., S-2-S.
    1 shelf, ¾ by 11½ by 15 in., S-2-S.
    1 shelf, ¾ by 12 by 15 in., S-2-S.
    1 shelf, ¾ by 14½ by 15 in., S-2-S.
    1 shelf, ¾ by 16 by 15 in., S-1-S.
    4 legs, ¾ by 5 by 41 in., S-2-S.
    2 lower crosspieces, ¾ by 3 by 9 in., S-2-S.
    2 upper crosspieces, ¾ by 2 by 9 in., S-2-S.
    4 end slats, ⅝ by 2 by 34 in., S-2-S.
    20 R.H. screws, 2 in. long.

The four shelves and the top are so wide that it will be necessary to make them from two or more pieces glued together. The top should have a ¼-in. bevel cut around the upper edge as shown in the drawing. The curve of the legs can be cut with a bracket saw

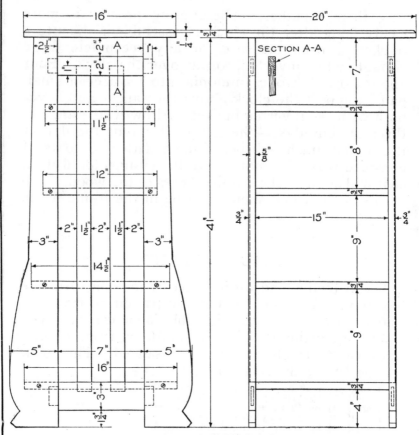

Details of Music Stand

or a drawknife, care being taken to get the edges square and smooth. The four crosspieces are fastened to the legs by means of tenons and mortises. The end slats are joined to the crosspieces in the same manner. The legs can be assembled in pairs with the slats and crosspieces in place. They can be glued in this position, and when dry they should be carefully gone

Music Stand Complete

over with fine sandpaper to remove all rough spots. The shelves can now be put in place. They should be fastened to the legs with round-headed screws. The top is also fastened on with screws. When applying the finish, remove the top board and the shelves and finish them separately. The stand can be finished in any one of the many mission stains supplied by the trade for this purpose.

This handsome piece of furniture can be used as a magazine stand as well as a music stand, if desired, and, if it is made and finished well, it will prove an ornament to any home.

MAKING SCREWS HOLD IN THE END GRAIN OF WOOD

It is often necessary to fasten one piece of wood to the end of another by means of screws. Wood being a fibrous material, it can be readily understood that when a screw having sharp threads is put in the end grain parallel to these fibers the threads cut them in such a way that, when an extra strain is put upon the parts, the screw pulls out, bringing with it the severed fibers. The accompanying sketch shows how this difficulty may be overcome, and at the same time make the screw hold firmly. A hole is bored and a dowel, preferably

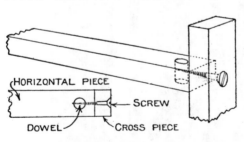

of hardwood, glued in it, the grain at right angles to that of the piece.

The size of the dowel, and its location, can be determined by the diameter and the length of the screw. The dowel need not extend all the way through the piece, but should be put in from the surface where the grain of the dowel will be least objectionable.

When putting screws in hard wood much labor will be saved by applying soap to the threads.

A WALL CASE WITH A MIRROR DOOR

The wall case shown in the accompanying picture will serve well as a medicine case. Having a paneled door in which is set a mirror, it serves equally well as a shaving case. It is best made of some hard wood, though a soft wood such as pine or yellow poplar will work up easier and look well finished with three or four coats of white enamel paint.

There will be needed the following pieces:

2 sides, 5/8 by 6 by 32 1/2 in., S-4-S.
1 top and 1 bottom, 5/8 by 6 by 18 in., S-4-S.
1 top of back, 1/2 by 4 by 16 1/4 in., S-2-S.
1 bottom of back, 1/2 by 3 by 16 1/4 in., S-4-S.
1 shelf, 5/8 by 5 by 16 in., S-4-S.
1 back, 1/4 by 16 by 21 in., S-2-S.

DOOR

2 stiles, 5/8 by 3 by 20 1/2 in., S-4-S.
1 top rail, 5/8 by 2 by 11 in., S-4-S.
1 bottom rail, 5/8 by 4 by 11 in., S-4-S.
1 backing for door, 3/16 by 10 by 15 in., S-2-S.

First shape the ends of the two side pieces as shown in the drawing. Next square the top and bottom pieces of the case to size, and lay out and cut the tenons on the ends. Lay out and cut the mortises in the side pieces, also the groove for the shelf, having **first** squared the shelf to size. Cut and shape the top **and** bottom pieces of the back as shown. Cut the rebates in the side pieces into which these pieces are to rest their ends. Cut the rebate for the back. Thoroughly scrape and sandpaper these parts and **assemble** them. Cut and fit the back in place.

Wall Case Details

The door is to be made next. Plan the different parts of the door so that the edges may be planed to fit the opening; that is, make the door a good quarter larger at top and bottom than the opening. In cutting the rebate the easiest way is to use a rabbeting plane and cut the full length of the pieces. By using a tenon on the rails in which one shoulder is as much longer than the other as the rebate is deep there is no resulting groove showing at the corner.

Case with Mirror Door

The wood should be finished before the glass is set, at least, it should be filled, if of hard wood, and one coat of paint put on, if of soft wood which is to be enameled.

In setting the glass, place a thin cushion of putty between the rebate and the glass and another thin cushion between the glass and the fillet of wood or the backing which is to protect the back of the glass.

Fit the door, and then put on the hinges and lock. If desired, the tenons may be made keyed as shown in the photograph instead of through as shown in the drawing.

To finish the case, if of oak, apply a coat of light paste filler, the directions being on the filler can. Next put on a coat of white shellac. When this has hardened apply two coats of some good varnish. Allow time for each coat to harden and rub the first coats with haircloth or curled hair, and the last with pulverized pumice and raw linseed oil or crude oil.

If the wood is soft and an enamel white is desired, the enamel is applied not unlike paint. The directions will be found on the cans in which the paint is purchased.

A SIDE CHAIR

A side chair of simple design and construction is here given. The great difficulty with most chair designs is that the back is generally designed narrower than the front, thus necessitating the rails entering the posts or legs at angles. To the amateur this is quite confusing. The chair illustrated is the same in width, both back and front, so that the shoulders of all the rails are at right angles to the sides. The back of the chair is straight, thus simplifying the design still more.

Another thing which is confusing to the beginner in his efforts to lay out the mortises is the irregular placing of the rails. It will be noted that in this

Side Chair Complete

design the rails of side, front and back are on the same level.

Plain sawed red oak will be appropriate for this piece. Have the pieces mill-planed and sandpapered

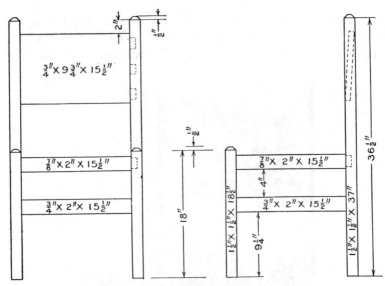

Details of Side Chair

on four sides to size, allowing ½ in. extra to the lengths for squaring up the ends.

There will be needed the following:

4 rails, ⅞ by 2 by 17½ in.
4 rails, ¾ by 2 by 17½ in.
2 front posts, 1½ by 1½ by 19 in.
2 rear posts, 1½ by 1½ by 37½ in.
1 back, ¾ by 9¾ by 17½ in.
2 cleats, ⅜ by 1 by 16 in.
4 slats, ⅜ by 2 by 16½ in.

Begin work by cutting the posts to the lengths indicated in the drawing. The lower ends should be chamfered slightly to prevent their splintering from usage. The top ends are cut to an angle of 45 deg., the slope beginning ½ in. below the top. Lay out and cut the mortises. To do this, lay off the measurements on one of the posts, then place all four side by side on the bench, with the face marks up.

Even the ends with the try-square and then carry the measurements just made across all of them, using the try-square. The rails ought to be shouldered on all four sides. Three-eighths inch is a good thickness for the tenons. The width may be 1¼ in. and the length 1 in.

Place the rails side by side on the bench with the joint-edges up and the ends evened. Measure off the desired length on one of them and carry the lines across all of them to indicate the location of the shoulder lines. Separate the pieces and square these lines entirely around all of the sides of each piece. With the tenon saw rip and cross cut to these lines.

The back, it will be noted, is set on a slant to add comfort. Thoroughly clean all the parts and assemble them, using good hot glue. Put the back together first, then the front. After these have dried, put the side rails in place.

Cut and fit the two cleats—one to the front rail and one to the rear rail. Keep them even with the lower edge of the rail so as to form a slight recess at the top when the slats are in place. This is to keep the cushion from sliding off. The slats need not be "let into" the cleats but merely fastened to their top edges. The cushion may be made of Spanish roan skin and should be filled with elastic felt.

In the chair shown, the joints are reinforced by the addition of lag screws. If the glue is good and the joints well fitted, these are not necessary.

AN ARM CHAIR

The arm chair here described and illustrated is intended to be one of the set of diners made after the design of the side chair described on another page. The same general directions for making the side chair apply equally to the arm chair.

The stock given in the following list should be purchased surfaced on four sides and well sandpapered:

2 rear posts, 1½ by 1½ by 38 in.
2 front posts, 1½ by 1½ by 26½ in.
9 rails, ⅞ by 2 by 19½ in.
1 rail, ⅞ by 1½ by 19½ in.
3 slats, ½ by 2 by 12½ in.
2 arms, ⅞ by 4½ by 20½ in.
2 brackets, ⅞ by 2¼ by 2½ in.
2 cleats, ⅜ by 1 by 19 in.
4 slats, ⅜ by 2 by 19 in.

Prepare the posts first by cutting them to the lengths shown in the drawing. In the photograph the front posts have their tops cut off square and the arms fastened to them by means of lag screws. A better way from a mechanical point of view would be to shoulder the top ends on the four sides, cut through-mortises in the arms and insert these tenoned posts into these mortises, pinning the arm to the post by means of small dowels in the edge of the post and through the tenon.

The brackets under the arms are to be fastened to the posts and arms by means of concealed dowels and glue of good quality.

All of the rails should be tenoned into the posts thoroughly, even if the lag screw fastenings are used. If the lag screws are used, the tenons may be what are known as stubb tenons—tenons of short length. Good hot glue should be used in either case.

The shape of the arms is indicated in the drawing
They are fastened to the rear posts by means of
dowels and glue.

Arm Chair Complete

The slats, or verticals, of the back should not have
their ends tenoned but should have the mortises in
the rails cut sufficiently large to "let in" the whole
end of each. This is much easier and more likely to
result in a satisfactory fit than to shoulder them.

Any unevenness in the lengths of the respective slats will not affect the fitting of the joints by this latter method.

The tops of the rear posts in this chair, as in the side chair, are cut to angles of 45 deg., beginning the slope at lines marked ½ in. from the tops.

The bottom is made up of 2-in. slats fitted between

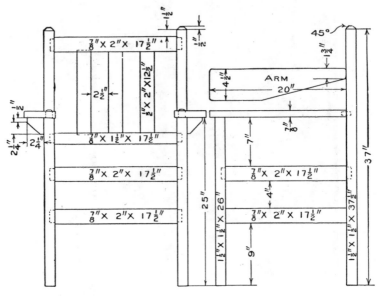

Details of Chair

the front and back rails and fastened to cleats which have been previously fastened to the insides of the front and back rails. Keep these cleats low enough on the rails so that the top surfaces of the slats shall rest somewhat below the top edges of the rails. Cushions, such as the one shown, can be purchased ready made or they can be easily made by the amateur.

A good finish for this chair and its mates is obtained as follows: Apply one coat of brown Flemish water stain. This stain in the original package is very dark in tone and unless an almost black finish is wanted, it should be lightened by the addition of one-half or two-thirds water. Apply with a brush or sponge and allow to dry over night. When dry, sandpaper lightly with fine or worn sandpaper to remove the raised grain caused by the water of the stain. Put on a very thin coat of shellac. This is to prevent the "high lights" in close-grained woods from being discolored by the stain in the filler which is to follow. The shellac being very thin does not fill the pores of the wood perceptibly. Next, sand the shellac coat lightly when it has hardened. Apply a coat of paste filler colored considerably darker than the stain to the tone desired for the open grain. If the filler is well stirred and properly applied, one coat ought to be sufficient. If it does not fill the pores satisfactorily, apply another coat when the first has had time to harden. Vandyke brown is used to color the filler, if none but natural color is to be had. On the hardened filler apply a thin coat of shellac. On this apply several coats of wax. The directions for waxing will be found upon the cans in which the wax comes.

A BOOKCASE

This beautiful piece of mission furniture can be made at a very moderate cost by anyone who has a slight knowledge of tools. Considerable labor can be saved by ordering the material from the mill ready cut to size, dressed and sanded. Quarter-sawed oak is the best wood to use and it is comparatively easy to obtain. Plain-sawed oak looks well, but is more liable to warp than the quarter-sawed and this is quite an element in pieces as wide as the ones used. For the complete bookcase the following material will be needed:

1 top, ¾ by 15 by 31¼ in., hard wood, S-1-S.
1 top back board, ¾ by 4 by 30¼ in., hard wood, S-1-S.
2 sides, ¾ by 14 by 50 in., hard wood, S-1-S.
1 bottom, ¾ by 14 by 28¾ in., hard wood, S-1-S.
1 bottom rail, ¾ by 4 by 28¾ in., hard wood, S-1-S.
1 center piece, ¾ by 2 by 45¾ in., hard wood, S-2-S.
4 door sides, ¾ by 1½ by 45¼ in., hard wood, S-2-S.
4 door ends, ¾ by 1½ by 14 in., hard wood, S-2-S.
4 pieces door lattice, ½ by ½ by 12½ in., hard wood.
4 pieces door lattice, ½ by ½ by 7 in., hard wood.
2 bottom cleats, 1¼ by 1¼ by 13 in., soft wood.
2 top cleats, 1 by 1 by 12½ in., soft wood.
3 shelves, ½ by 12 by 28½ in., soft wood.
12 pieces backing, ⅜ by 4 by 29¾ in., soft wood.
4 hinges.
2 door handles.

Begin with the sides by cutting them so they will pair up all right. The front edges are rounded while the back edges are rabbeted on the inside as deep as the backing to be used. The bottoms are cut as shown in the sketch. Holes about ½ in. deep should be bored on the inside at the proper places for the wooden pegs which hold up the shelves.

The top and bottom boards should have the front edges rounded and sanded the same as the sides.

Completed Bookcase.

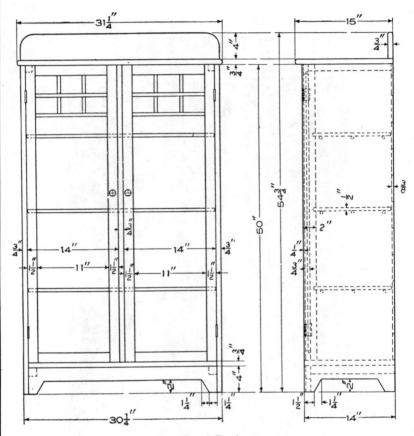

Details of Bookcase

The top board is sanded on one side only and care should be taken to get the best side up.

Now cut and fit the top back board. This is fastened to the top by means of screws. Screw two cleats to each of the sides as shown and by running screws through these into the top and bottom boards the frame is completed.

The backing which can be made of some cheap lumber is now put on. Next put in the center upright piece between the doors by means of a tenon and mortise at the top and nail at the bottom. The front edge should be rounded and the edge and sides sanded. Cut and fit the bottom rail as shown. It is fastened to the frame by means of cleats on the back side.

The doors are put together by means of a tenon and mortise. They should be rabbeted for the lattice work and the glass. This lattice work can be omitted and leaded glass put in its place which is very becoming to this kind of work.

When the case is completed it must be carefully gone over with sandpaper before any finish is applied.

A mission stain is suitable for work of this kind, but it can also be finished in "golden oak" which is done in the following manner: First put on a golden oak stain and after it has dried for about 2 hours, apply the filler. Let this dry about 10 minutes then rub off with an old rag. Then go over the case again with some very fine sandpaper and after seeing that all parts are free from dust and dirt the varnish can be applied. Three coats of varnish will give a beautiful glossy finish.

A LAMP STAND

A mission table lamp stand for those who use electric lights is shown in the accompanying illustration. It is suitable for either the office or the home and is very simple in design and construction. The stock should be quarter-sawed oak and it can be

ordered from the mill ready cut to **length, squared**
and sanded. The following pieces will be needed:

1 post, 1½ in. sq. by 23 in.
1 arm, 1⅛ by ¾ by 13½ in.
1 block, ¾ in. thick by 6 in. square.
1 block, 1 in. thick by 9 in. square.

Square up the base blocks and fasten them to-

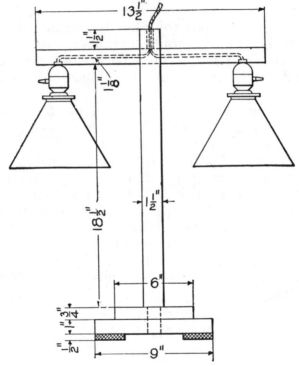

Details of Lamp Stand

gether with screws as shown in the detail sketch. A
mortise, 1 in. square, is cut in the center of the blocks
for the center post. Lead weights, covered with felt,

should be attached to the bottom, as shown. The post has a tenon cut on one end to fit the base, and a mortise cut in the other for the arm. Holes are bored in the arm from the ends for the wires. They can be plugged after the wires are in place. A hole

Electric Lamp Stand Complete

is also bored in the top of the center post to connect with the holes in the arm for the lead wire.

It is best to glue the joints together, although this is not necessary if the joints are a tight fit. Sandpaper the parts thoroughly, then stain to match the other furniture.

Extension Dining Table Complete

AN EXTENSION DINING TABLE

The accompanying sketch and photograph show a simple design of an extension dining table of the mission style. It is very easy to construct and can be built at home by anyone who is at all handy with tools. It should be made of quarter-sawed oak, which can be secured at the mill ready cut to length, squared and sanded. Order the following pieces:

```
 2 top pieces, 1 by 23 by 46 in.
 2 extra leaves, 1 by 12 by 46 in.
 2 rails, 3/4 by 3 by 44 in.
 4 rails, 3/4 by 3 by 22 in.
 2 pieces for posts, 3/4 by 8 by 24 in.
 2 pieces for posts, 3/4 by 6 by 24 in.
 4 pieces for feet, 3 by 3 by 14 in.
 4 pieces for feet, 3 by 3 by 5 in.
 4 pieces for feet, 1 by 4 by 4 in.
 4 pieces moulding, 1 by 1 by 10 in.
 1 piece, 1 by 12 by 27 in., birchwood.
 2 brackets, 3/4 by 3 by 32 in., birchwood.
 2 pieces for slide, 1 3/4 by 3 by 36 in., birchwood.
 4 pieces for slide, 1 by 3 by 36 in., birchwood.
12 pieces for slide, 3/4 by 1 1/2 by 36 in., birchwood.
```

The feet can be made first by squaring up one end of each and beveling the other as shown in the drawing. The short pieces are fastened to the long ones by means of long screws and glue. The four square pieces should be nailed to the outer ends and holes bored in them for the casters. Prepare the pieces for the posts, and before nailing them together fasten the feet to them with long screws. Be careful to get them on square, else the table will not set level when complete. Now nail and glue the pieces forming the table together and fasten the moulding at the bottom. This moulding should have mitered corners as shown in the bottom view. Also fasten the rest piece to the top of the post, using long screws and glue.

The slides can be made next. The pieces are made

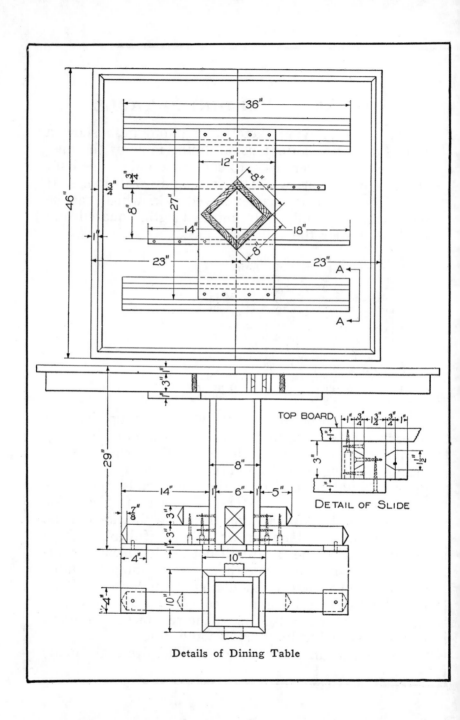

Details of Dining Table

and fastened together with screws as shown in the enlarged detail view. This slide, if made with care, is a good one. The center piece should be firmly fastened to the post rest with long screws. The screws that fasten into the top should be inserted from below through counter-bored holes as shown.

Miter the rails at the corners and glue them to the top. Blocks can be used on the inside if desired, which will make a much stronger construction. Screw the two brackets to the top as shown. These help to support the table when it is extended.

When complete the table should be carefully gone over with fine sandpaper, and all glue and rough spots removed. Apply stain of the desired color. This can be any one of the many mission stains supplied by the trade for this purpose.

AN OAK-BOUND CEDAR CHEST

This cedar chest for storing unused bedding or furs is not a difficult thing to make and when made, the hard oak binding takes the wear and protects the softer cedar so that the chest ought to serve several generations. Order the stock as follows:

CEDAR
2 top and bottom pieces, ⅞ by 16½ by 34½ in., S-2-S.
2 sides, ⅞ by 18⅞ by 34½ in., S-2-S.
2 ends, ⅞ by 18⅞ by 14¾ in., S-2-S.
OAK
2 overhanging top pieces, 1 by 1 by 36½ in., S-4-S.
2 overhanging top pieces, 1 by 1 by 18½ in., S-4-S.
2 lock and hinge rails, 1 by 2½ by 36½ in., S-2-S.
2 lock and hinge rails, 1 by 2½ by 18½ in., S-2-S.
2 base pieces, 1 by 3¼ by 36½ in., S-2-S.
2 base pieces, 1 by 3¼ by 18½ in., S-2-S.

Specify thoroughly seasoned Tennessee red cedar

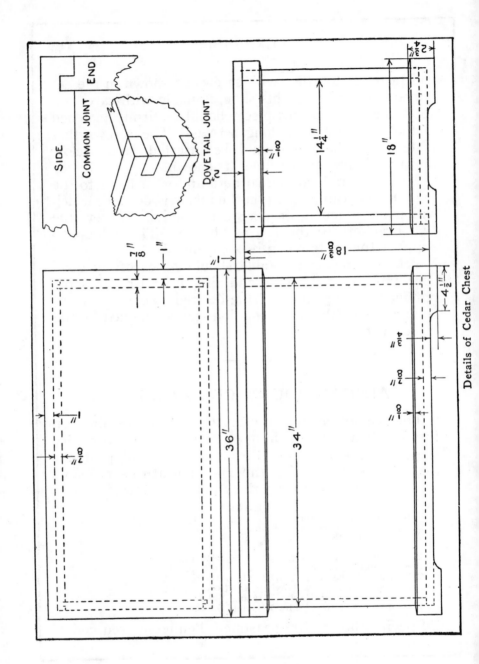

Details of Cedar Chest

and plain sawed white oak and have the different pieces millplaned and sandpapered as indicated in the stock-bill. This bill allows ½ in. extra on the length and the width of each piece for "squaring up" of all pieces except those marked to be surfaced on four sides.

Begin by squaring the sides and ends to size. Probably the best joint for the corners is the dovetail. If the worker is not experienced in woodworking, some of the more simple joints will do. It will be noted that the drawing and stock-bill call for the simplest form of joint, that in which the sides of the chest lap over the end. For the dovetail joint it will be necessary to add 2 in. more to the length of the end pieces, making them 16¾ in. each in the rough.

Having got the sides and ends ready, fasten them together. The perspective shows the sides fastened to the ends with ornamental headed nails. Common nails are first used, being equally spaced, and the ornamental heads are afterwards placed so as to cover their heads.

Next square the bottom and nail it to the parts just assembled. Square the top to the same size.

The base stuff is squared on one edge only. The second edge—the upper one—is to be beveled or sloped ⅛ in. to facilitate dusting and for appearance sake. Fit these base pieces to place, mitering the joints. Before fastening the parts to the chest proper, gauge a line ¾ in. from the lower edge and to a point 4½ in. from each end, cut out to this line and shape the base as shown in the drawing. Use finishing nails for fastening the base to the chest. The heads should be "set" so they may be covered later with a putty colored to match the finish.

In a similar manner plane up, cut and fit the back and hinge rails. These rails should be kept a "scant" ⅛ in. below the top edges of the chest proper. The overhang of the lid fits down over in such a way as to form a dust-proof joint between lid and chest proper.

The overhang of the lid of 1 in. by 1-in. stock may next be mitered, fitted and nailed to the lid. Thoroughly sandpaper all parts not so treated and finish as follows: Put on all the oak pieces, two coats of natural paste filler. This is best done before they are fastened in place. Directions will be found on the cans in which the filler is kept.

The red of the cedar may be heightened by applying a mahogany stain made of Bismark brown aniline and boiling water, in the proportion of 3 qt. of water to 1 oz. of aniline. If applied hot the stain will enter the wood better. When dry, sandpaper lightly with No. 00 paper, both this and the oak-filled pieces.

Fasten the oak pieces in place and give the whole exterior a very thin coat of shellac. After this has hardened, apply two coats of wax. Wax comes in paste form and is to be applied with a cloth very sparingly. Allow it to stand five or ten minutes then rub briskly with a soft dry cloth to polish. The first coat is allowed to stand 24 hours before the second is applied in a similar manner.

Another finish, known as an egg-shell gloss shellac finish, is obtained by omitting the wax and instead applying from two to five more coats of shellac. Allow each coat 24 hours in which to harden, and rub each hardened coat to a smooth finish, using curled hair, or fine steel wool, or fine oiled sandpaper, before applying the next.

The metal reinforcements for the corners can be bought at a hardware store, as can the lock, hinges,

Cedar Chest Complete

and handles. These parts are applied in the usual manner—butt hinges being used.

If well made, the chest is practically airtight. The interior is all of red cedar, while the effect of the exterior in combining the light oak and the red cedar is striking.

A TOOL FOR MAKING MORTISES

In the construction of mission furniture where mortise joints are mostly used, those who cannot have access to a mortising machine will find the following method of great assistance in obtaining a true mortise, which is necessary in work of this kind.

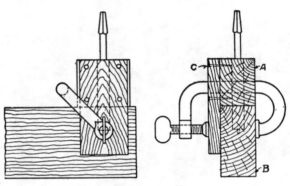

Boring Holes for Tenons

Take a block of wood, A, the exact thickness of the piece B to be mortised, and with an auger bore a hole, the same size as the width of the mortise to be made, exactly parallel to the sides of the block. This can best be done on a drill press or a wood boring machine. If no machine is available, great care should be taken in boring by hand, to get the hole as nearly true as possible. Then nail a cleat, C, on the side of the block, A, and let it extend down on piece B. Use a clamp to hold the block in place while boring out the mortise. By changing the position of the block and boring a number of holes, any length of mortise can be made. The holes should afterwards be squared up with a chisel.

A DRESSER FOR CHILD'S PLAYROOM

This dresser can be made of two kinds of wood as marked on the drawing or it can be made all of one kind. The original dresser was made of oak and walnut and was finished natural, the contrast between the light and dark woods adding much to the value of the piece in the eyes of the little ones. Have all surfaces that will show well sandpapered at the mill. The following is a list of the material wanted:

4 oak posts, 1½ in. square by 19½ in., S-4-S.
3 walnut drawer fronts, ¾ by 5 by 17 in., S-2-S.
6 yellow poplar drawer sides, ⅜ by 5 by 12 in., S-2-S.
3 yellow poplar backs, ⅜ by 4½ by 16½ in., S-2-S.
3 yellow poplar bottoms, ⅜ by 12 by 16½ in., S-2-S.
4 oak front stretchers, ⅞ by 1¾ by 17½ in., S-4-S.
4 oak side rails, ⅞ by 2 by 12 in., S-4-S.
2 walnut side panels, ¼ by 11 by 14½ in., S-2-S.
8 oak drawer slides, ⅞ by 2 by 10½ in., S-2-S.
6 oak drawer guides, ½ by ¾ by 10½ in., S-2-S.
4 oak back stretchers, ⅞ by 2 by 17½ in., S-2-S.
1 oak top, ⅝ by 14 by 20½ in., S-2-S.
3 sq. ft. of ⅜ in. matched yellow pine ceiling for back.

MIRROR SUPPORT
1 walnut piece, ⅞ by 1¾ by 20½ in., S-2-S.
1 walnut piece, ⅞ by 1½ by 18 in., S-2-S.
1 oak piece, ¾ by 1¼ by 10½ in., S-2-S.
2 oak pieces, ⅞ by 1½ by 11 in., S-2-S.
1 walnut bracket piece, ⅞ by 1¼ by 5 in., S-2-S.

MIRROR FRAME PARTS
2 walnut pieces, ⅞ by 1½ by 12½ in., S-2-S.
2 walnut pieces, ⅞ by 1½ by 10½ in., S-2-S.
2 oak pieces, ¼ by ⅜ by 10 in., S-4-S.
2 oak pieces, ¼ by ⅜ by 8 in., S-4-S.
1 back, ³⁄₁₆ by 8 by 10 in., soft wood.
2 cleats, ⅜ by 1¼ by 8 in.
1 plain mirror glass, 7½ by 9½ in.

Begin by planing the four posts to length. The lower ends should be slightly beveled to prevent their slivering. Cut the mortises for the tenons that are on the ends of the side rails. These rails are to be ⅞ by 2 in. and the tenons should be ⅜ by 1¼ in. wide by ¾ in. long. The posts should be rabbeted down

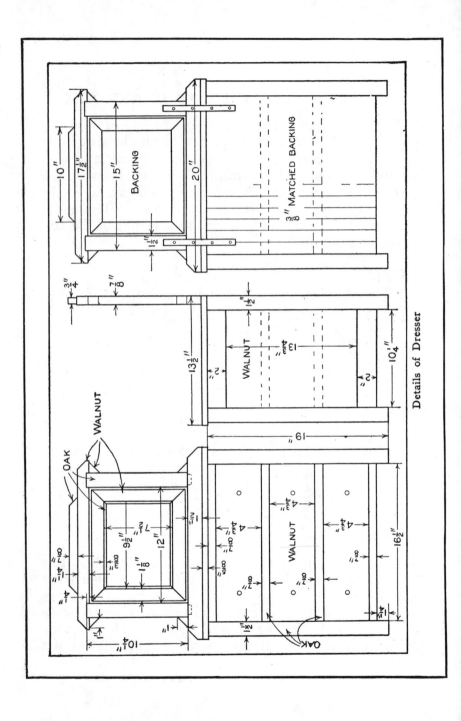

Details of Dresser

to their middles to a depth of ⅜ in. so as to receive
the ¼-in. end panels. The end rails should be cut to

Dresser Complete

length and their tenons worked after one edge of each
has been rabbeted as were the posts.

Having squared the panels to size, put the two ends of the dresser together with glue. Next make the four frames which are to carry the drawers. They should measure from outside to outside, in length 17½ in.; in width, 12½ in. It is intended that the short pieces shall be tenoned into the long ones. When these frames are ready, cut out each corner as indicated in the cross section drawing. Reduce to size the drawer guides and fasten them in place. Dowel the frames to the ends of the dresser in the places indicated on the drawing. Put on the back, nailing into frames to the ends of the dresser in the places indi- and fasten the top in place, putting screws into it from the under side.

The mirror frame and support should next be made. The drawing shows quite clearly the parts and their relation to each other. All the slopes are of 45 deg. Instead of rabbeting the mirror frame, a ¼ by ⅜-in. fillet of oak is nailed around to form the recess, the walnut frame and oak fillet making a pretty contrast. All nail holes are to be filled with putty colored to match the finish. Wooden pins or round-head screws are to be used to fasten the mirror frame to its support and should be placed above center an inch or so.

The drawers are to be constructed in the usual manner. It is a good plan to make the grooves 1/16 in. narrower than the stock is thick to insure a fit, chamfering the under or back sides of the bottom and back if necessary. Make the sides of the drawers of such a length that when the drawer has been pushed in as far as it will go, the front will be recessed about ¼ in. behind the front crosspieces. Groove the inside of the drawer front $\frac{3}{16}$ in. to receive the bottom. The mirror should not be placed until the wood has been finished.

Finish the wood natural, apply three coats of varnish. Rub the first two with haircloth or curled hair and the last with pulverized pumice stone and crude oil or raw linseed oil. This gives an egg-shell gloss.

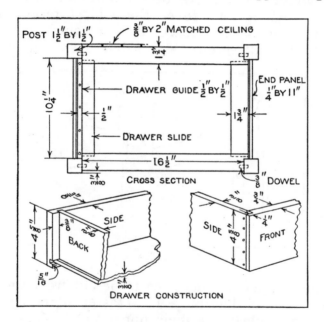

CROSS SECTION

DRAWER CONSTRUCTION

For a dull finish, rub the varnish after it has become bone dry with pulverized pumice stone and water, using a piece of rubbing felt. Rub until the surface is smooth and even, and clean with a wet sponge or chamois skin. If a polished finish is desired, rub first with pulverized pumice stone and water, then with rotten stone and water. Finish with a mixture of oil and a little pulverized rotten stone.

CUTTING TENONS WITH A HAND-SAW

This home-made tool will be a great help in the construction of mission furniture. With its use, tenons may be entirely cut with a saw, discarding the use of a chisel and mallet. The device consists of a convenient length of straight board, A, Fig. 1, wide enough to cover the widest piece to be tenoned. A piece of board, B, is fastened to A with brads or small screws. This board should have a

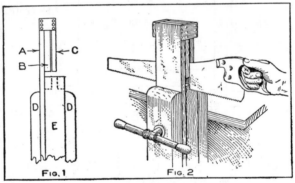

Sawing Tenons

thickness equal to the piece to be cut from the side of the tenon. The piece C is fastened to A and B with small cleats at their upper ends. The space between B and C should be wide enough for the blade of a saw to run through easily, and also long enough to take in the widest part of the saw blade. The tool and piece to be tenoned are placed in a vise as shown in Fig. 2. The width of the piece removed for the tenon may be varied by putting in pieces of cardboard between the work, E, and the piece A, Fig. 1.

ARTS AND CRAFTS OIL LAMP

Electricity and gas are not always accessible in suburban or country homes and the regular type of a mission lamp would be of little use. The illustration

Artistic Mission Style Oil Lamp

shows an ordinary round wick kerosene lamp fitted out in mission style.

A few modifications were made in the design of an expensive lamp to simplify the construction. The lamp should have a tall chimney. The dimensions given in the drawings, and the photograph, will ex-

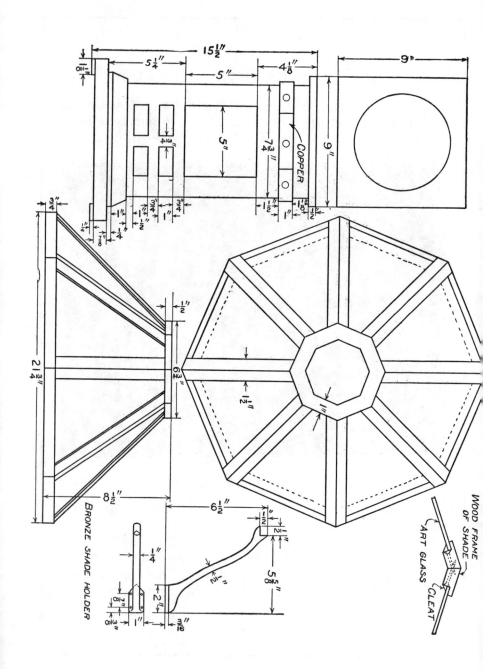

BRONZE SHADE HOLDER

COPPER

WOOD FRAME OF SHADE

ART GLASS

CLEAT

plain themselves. Many of the details can be worked up by the maker.

The body of the lamp is made of ½-in. oak and is provided with openings as shown. The interior receptacle is very handy for holding a match box, smoking articles, etc.

A piece of copper band, 1 in. wide, is fastened to the body with large upholsterers' tacks, to give it a finished appearance. The base is ⅞ in. thick and in order to prevent tilting is provided with four square feet, ¼ in. thick. The top piece of the body is ½-in. oak, which is provided with a hole large enough to receive the bowl of the lamp. If such a lamp is not at hand, one can be purchased at a very reasonable price.

The shade is made of oak frames set in with clouded art glass panels. The different sections of the frames are fastened together with brass screws and the glass is held in place by triangular cleats of oak. Be sure and fit the shade with cardboard panels before ordering the glass. The cardboard can be used as a pattern in cutting the glass, and the glass will then fit without recutting, which is quite difficult.

The glass beaded fringe should be of suitable color to harmonize with the finished lamp.

The shade is supported by four brackets cast in bronze from a wood pattern (dimensions given) and finished by filing, buffing and lacquering.

ANOTHER CHINA CLOSET

The china closet shown in the accompanying illustration is well proportioned and of pleasing appearance. It can be made of any one of the several furniture woods in common use, but quarter-sawed oak will be found to give the most pleasing effect. The stock should be ordered from the mill ready sawed to length, squared and sanded. In this way much hard labor will be saved. The following pieces will be needed:

```
1 top, 1 by 19 by 38 in., S-1-S.
4 posts, ¾ by 3 by 59 in., S-2-S.
4 side rails, ¾ by 3 by 31 in., S-1-S.
4 end uprights, 1 by 2 by 48½ in., S-2-S.
4 end rails, 1 by 3 by 16 in., S-2-S.
2 lattice rails, 1 by 2 by 13 in., S-2-S.
1 top board, ¾ by 3 by 36 in., S-1-S.
4 side door rails, ¾ by 2 by 47 in., S-2-S.
6 cross rails, ¾ by 2 by 12 in., S-2-S.
4 slats, ½ by ¾ by 16½ in., S-2-S.
4 slats, ½ by ¾ by 13½ in., S-2-S.
8 slats, ½ by ¾ by 12½ in., S-2-S.
4 shelves, ⅝ by 16 by 32 in., S-1-S., poplar.
4 cleats, 1 in. sq. by 55 in., soft wood.
4 cleats, 1 in. sq. by 28 in., soft wood.
4 cleats, 1 in. sq. by 14 in., soft wood.
```

Having this material on hand, start with the four posts, as they are all alike. Clamp them together, being careful to have them of the right length, and the ends square. Trim the bottom, as shown in the detail drawing, and then lay out the mortises for the front and back rails. These rails can now be laid out and the tenons cut to fit the mortises in the posts. The back rails should, in addition, be rabbeted for the back board as shown. The end rails are fastened to the posts by means of screws through 1-in. square cleats, fastened on the inside of the posts as shown in the section A-A. In all cases the screws

China Closet with Latticework Doors and Sides

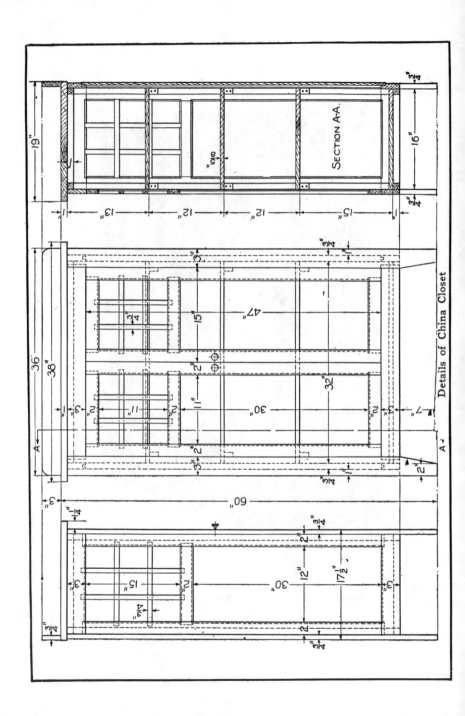

Details of China Closet

should be run through the cleats into the framing so the heads will not show. The end rails should be rabbeted on the inside for the latticework and the glass.

The back board should have the corners rounded as shown and be fastened to the top board with screws through from the bottom side. The top board is then fastened to the top rail cleats in the same manner.

The doors are put together by means of tenons and mortises. The frames should be rabbeted on the inside for the latticework and the glass. Leaded glass can be used in place of this latticework, if it is desired. Suitable hinges and a catch should be supplied. These can be purchased at any hardware store.

The shelves should be cut out at the corners to fit around the cleats. They rest on small blocks which are fastened to the cleats, or if desired, small holes can be drilled and pins used instead.

The back is put on in the usual manner. A mirror can be put in without much trouble if it is desired.

When putting the frame together, glue should be used on the joints, as it makes them much stiffer. Be careful to get the frame together perfectly square, or it will be hard to fit the doors and the glass. When it is complete, go over the whole carefully with fine sandpaper and remove all rough spots. Scrape all the surplus glue from about the joints, as stain will not take when there is any glue. The closet can be finished in any one of the many mission stains supplied by the trade for this purpose.

Oak Bedstead Complete

AN OAK BEDSTEAD

The accompanying sketches show an artistic design for a mission bed, so simple in construction and design that most any one that has a few tools and a knowledge of their use can make it. It is best made of quarter-sawed oak, as this wood is the easiest to procure and work up and looks well with any finish. If the stock is ordered from the mill ready cut to length, squared and sanded, much of the hard labor will be saved.

The following is a list of the material needed:

2 posts, 2½ by 2½ by 50 in.
2 posts, 2½ by 2½ by 44 in.
2 end rails, 1 by 6 by 56 in.
2 side rails, 1 by 6 by 78 in.
5 end rails, 1 by 4 by 56 in.
3 end rails, 1 by 2 by 56 in.
8 vertical slats, ⅜ by 6 by 11½ in.
10 vertical slats, ⅜ by 2 by 11½ in.
2 cleats, 1 by 1 by 78 in.
5 slats, ¾ by 3 by 55½ in.
20 blocks, 1 by 1 by 3 in.

Square up the four posts in pairs and lay out the mortises as per drawing. To do this, lay them side by side on a flat surface with the ends square and mark them with a try-square. The tenons on the end rails are laid out in the same manner as the posts. Four of the end rails should be marked and mortises cut for the upright slats as shown in the detail drawing. The tenons on the end rails are about 1 in. long, while those on the slats can be ¾ in. long. Fit all the parts together before gluing to see that they fit square and tight. After the glue has been applied clamp them together perfectly square and set them away to dry. They should dry at least twenty-four hours before the clamps are removed.

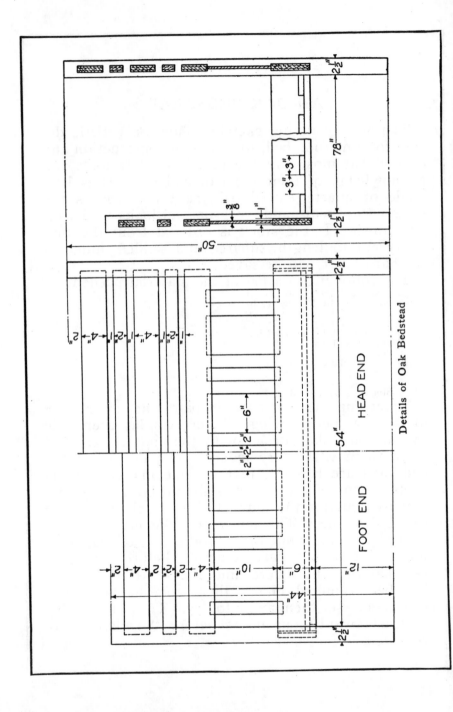

Details of Oak Bedstead

While the ends are drying, the side rails can be made. These have a 1-in. square cleat screwed to the inner side for the slats to rest upon. If springs are used, five slats will be sufficient. They can be placed where the springs will rest upon them. After the position of the slats has been located, nail small blocks at their sides to hold them in place. For fastening the side rails to the posts, patent devices can be purchased at a local hardware store. The posts will have to be mortised to receive these, and care should be exercised to get them in the right place.

When the bed is complete go over it carefully and scrape all the surplus glue from about the joints, as the finish will not take where there is any glue. Remove all rough spots with fine sandpaper; then apply the stain you like best, which may be any of the many mission stains supplied by the trade for this purpose. If this bed is well made and finished, it will be an ornament to any home.

AN OAK FOOTSTOOL

The footstool shown in the illustration can be made from any kind of wood, but when it is intended to be finished in mission style, quarter-sawed oak will produce the best effect. The material needed will be as follows:

1 top, 1 by 9½ by 12 in., S-1-S.
2 legs, ¾ by 8 by 12 in., S-2-S.
1 brace, ¾ by 7 by 9 in., S-1-S.

Order these pieces cut to length, squared and sanded. A full-sized layout of the front view should be made to get the correct bevels for the legs and brace. The design of the legs can be varied to suit the fancy of the maker. For such a design as shown draw one-half of it on paper; fold on the center line and with scissors cut both sides of the outline by following the lines

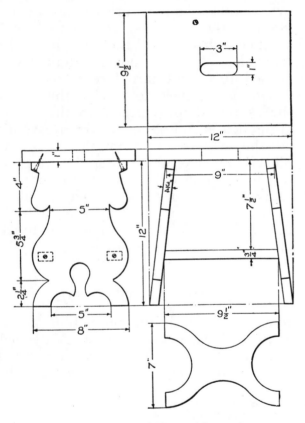

Details of Footstool

drawn. Trace around this pattern on the wood, and saw out with a compass or keyhole saw. The sawed edges should be smoothed and sandpapered.

The perforation in the top board is made by first boring holes, then trimming out the edges with a sharp chisel. Be sure to get the best side of the board up.

The legs are fastened to the top and to the braces with 1¾-in. wood screws as shown in the detail draw-

Footstool Complete

ing. After the stool is assembled, go over it carefully with fine sandpaper and remove all rough spots before applying the finish. This finish can be any one of the many different kinds supplied by the trade for this purpose. If this stool is well made and finished, it will be a useful and attractive article.

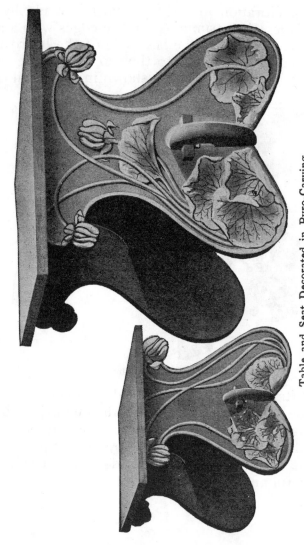

Table and Seat Decorated in Pyro-Carving

A LIBRARY SET IN PYRO-CARVING

The multitude of indifferently executed small articles which followed the introduction of pyrography is beginning to disappear, people are considering the art more seriously and applying it to more dignified uses. Pyro-carving is one of the new methods of decorating furniture which is both beautiful and practical, two qualities which do not always go together.

The library set illustrated consists of a table, 30 by 50 in., with two benches, 14 in. wide of the same length. The supports are made of selected white pine, which must be absolutely free from pitch. The pine is soft enough to work easily with the point and stands wear much better than basswood. The tops and braces are made of curly fir, all of the material must be 2-in. lumber, which dresses to about an inch and a half. All surfaces, except the faces of the supports, are given a well-rubbed coat of oil with a little burnt umber, the stain to be applied directly to the wood without a filler.

On the outside of the supports the design is drawn in with pencil, the background is then cut out smoothly with a chisel to the depth of an eighth of an inch, leaving the decoration in relief. It is then burned deeply, the background in straight flat strokes, the outlines having the effect of a sloping, dark edge. The shadows are burned in as deeply as possible and the shading is put in with the flat of the point.

A wax or egg-shell oil varnish finish is most suitable for this set.

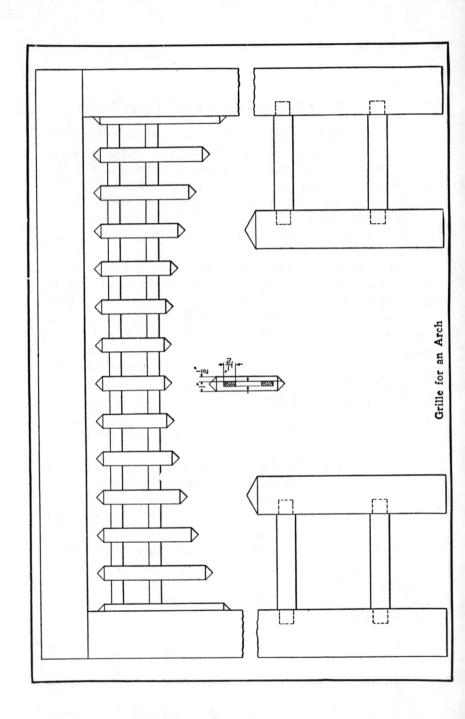

Grille for an Arch

A GRILLE WITH PEDESTALS TO MATCH

The accompanying sketch shows something unique in a grille that adds to the appearance of a home furnished in mission style. When it is stained and finished to match the furniture, it gives a consummate tone that would be difficult to obtain by any other means.

To get the best results it should be made to blend with the furniture and the arch in which it is to fit, in both weight and style. This will depend very much upon one's preference, and for this reason full dimensions are not given. No difficulty will be experienced, however, by anyone handy with tools, in making it.

The material should be quarter-sawed oak, which can be secured planed and sanded at the mill. For the grille order 1 by 1½-in. and ½ by 1½-in. stock. The method of making the bars is shown in the detailed sketch. The two end bars should be made of solid pieces, ¾ by 1½ in., with two rectangular slots mortised in each to receive the supports. The supports should be just the right length to go in the arch. To erect, slip the end bars on the supports, hold the grille in place and fasten the bars to the sides of the arch with screws.

The size of the pedestals and the connecting pieces will depend upon the size of the arch. These connecting pieces should be well mortised into the post, and if you own your own home and intend the pedestals to become a fixture, they should also be mortised into the sides of the arch. If not, they may be fastened to the arch with blind screws. The amount of material required will depend upon the size of the arch.

A LADY'S WRITING DESK

This desk of mission style is a little more complicated than some of the other pieces of mission furniture that have been described, but anyone who has a fair knowledge of tools will not have much trouble in constructing it in the home workshop if the plans are carefully followed. Quarter-sawed oak is the best wood to use, as it is easy to work and looks best when finished. Order the stock from the mill ready cut to length, squared and sanded. Following is a list of the stock needed:

2 front posts, 2 by 2 by 30 in.
2 back posts, 2 by 2 by 50 in.
1 bottom rail, ¾ by 3 by 31 in.
2 end rails, ¾ by 3 by 18 in.
1 stretcher, ¾ by 8 by 33½ in.
2 end slats, ⅜ by 8 by 15 in.
1 back slat, ⅜ by 8 by 15½ in.
2 back slats, ⅜ by 3 by 15½ in.
1 front drawer rail, ¾ by 1¼ by 31¼ in.
2 side drawer rails, ¾ by 3 by 18¼ in.
1 drawer front, ¾ by 6 by 30 in.
1 desk lid, ¾ by 18 by 31¼ in.
1 desk board, ¾ by 19¼ by 31¼ in.
2 end boards, ¾ by 19 by 21¼ in.
1 top board, ¾ by 10 by 34 in.
1 top back board, ¾ by 5 by 31¼ in.
1 back board, ¾ by 30 by 22 in.
2 drawer sides, ½ by 6 by 19½ in., S. W.
1 drawer end, ½ by 6 by 29 in., S. W.
1 drawer bottom, ½ by 18 by 29 in., S. W.
2 pieces for pigeon holes, ⅜ by 7 by 23 in., S. W.
8 pieces for pigeon holes, ⅜ by 4 by 6¾ in., S. W.

Start with the back posts, being sure they are square and of the right length; place them side by side and lay out the mortises for the lower rails, the desk rails and the top back boards, as shown in the accompanying detail drawing. Lay out the front posts in the same manner. Cut the tenons on the ends of the rails to fit the mortises in the posts.

Also cut mortises in the rails for the back and end slats. The end rails have a mortise in them for the tenons on the ends of the foot boards. Clamp the ends of the desk together, with the end rails in place; then fit the side boards. Bore holes through

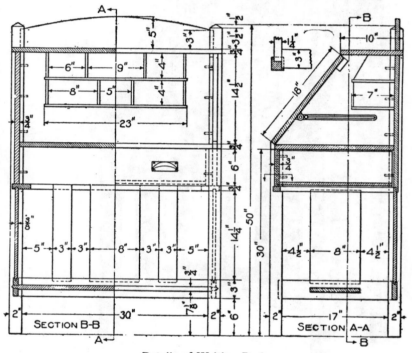

Details of Writing Desk

the posts into the side boards for dowels as shown. After the dowels are in place the holes can be plugged.

Cut and fit the top back board, the bottom rail, the back board and the stretcher. Cut the top and desk boards at the back corners to clear the posts.

The top board is to be fastened to the side boards with blind screws. The back board is fastened to the posts with dowels as shown.

When all the parts fit square and tight they can

Desk Complete

be glued together. The ends of the desk should be glued up first and left to dry, then the other parts put in place and glued. When clamping the parts together see that they fit perfectly square and tight.

While the glue is drying the drawer can be made. The front board is made of oak, but the other parts may be made of some soft wood. The side pieces are mortised and glued to the front board. The end and bottom boards can be nailed together.

The drop lid of the desk is made as shown. Two or more boards may have to be glued together for the lid, the desk bottom and the back board. The lid is fastened to the desk board with two hinges, and it should be so arranged that when closed it will be even with the sides. Brackets or chains are fastened to the inside to hold it in the proper position when it is open. Small blocks of wood fastened to the inner edge of the side boards will prevent it from closing too far. A lock, if desired, can be purchased at a hardware store and fitted in place. Suitable handles for the drawer should also be provided.

When the desk is complete go over it with fine sandpaper and remove all rough spots. Scrape all glue from about the joints, as the finish will not take where there is any glue.

The pigeonholes are made from ⅜-in. stock. They may be tacked in place after the desk is finished.

The finish can be any one of the many mission stains supplied by the trade for this purpose. If the desk is well made and finished, it will have a very neat and attractive appearance.

A TELEPHONE STAND AND STOOL

The stand shown in the accompanying illustration is for use with a desk telephone. The stool when not in use, slides on two runners under the stand.

Stand and Stool Complete

A shelf is provided for the telephone directory, paper, pencil, etc.

The joints may be made with dowels, or the mortise and tenon may be used, as desired. If the latter is decided upon, allowance must be made on the length of the rails for the tenons.   The list given is for the dowel-made joints.   The following stock list

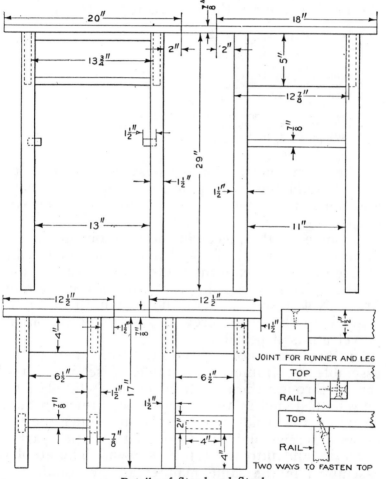

Details of Stand and Stool

gives the amount of material needed which should be ordered planed and sanded.   This work can be done by hand if the builder has the time and desires to have an entire home-made article. However, the list is given for the mill-planed material.

STAND

4 posts, 1½ in. square by 29 in.
2 rails, ⅞ by 5 by 11 in.
1 rail, ⅞ by 1½ by 13 in.
1 rail, ⅞ by 5 by 13 in.
2 runners, ⅞ by 1½ by 14 in.
1 top, ⅞ by 18 by 20 in.
1 shelf, ⅞ by 12⅞ by 13¾ in.

STOOL

4 posts, 1½ in. square by 17 in.
4 rails, ⅞ by 4 by 6½ in.
4 rails, ⅞ by 2 by 6½ in.
1 stretcher, ⅞ by 4 by 7¼ in.
1 top, ⅞ by 12½ in. square.

The exact lengths for the posts are given in the list. Should the builder desire to square them up, allowance must be made for this when ordering stock.

Arrange all the pieces in the position they are to occupy in the finished stand and stool and number all the joints. Locate the centers and bore holes for all the dowels. Assemble the two sides of the table first. Notch the runners and fasten them to the posts with flat-head screws. Use hot glue on the dowel joints if possible.

Cut the corners out of the shelf to fit the legs and assemble the frame of the table. Use round-head screws through the rails to hold the shelf. The top may be fastened in two ways, with screws through cleats on the inside of the rails and under the top, or with screws slanting through the upper part of the rails and into the top as shown. The stool is assembled in the same manner as the stand.

The stand and stool should be finished to harmonize with the furniture and woodwork of the room in which they are to be used.

HOW TO MAKE A DOWEL-CUTTING TOOL

Secure a piece of steel about ¼ in. thick, 1¾ in. wide and 8 in. long. Drill various sized holes through the steel as shown in Fig. 1, leaving the edge of each hole as sharp as the drill will make them. Cut off a block of wood the length necessary

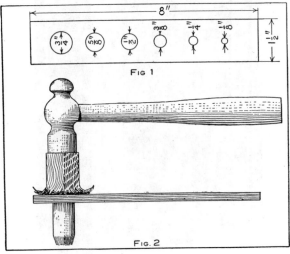

Easy Way to Make Dowels

for the dowels and split it up into pieces about the size for the particular dowel to be used. Lay the steel on something flat, over a hole of some kind, then start one of the pieces of wood in the proper size hole for the dowel and drive it through with a hammer, as shown in Fig. 2. The sharp edges on the steel will cut the dowel as smooth and round as if it were turned in a lathe.

A MEDICINE CABINET

This cabinet is best made of quarter-sawed oak, as this wood is the most easily procured and looks well when finished. Order the stock from the mill ready

Medicine Cabinet Complete

cut to length, squared and sanded. The following pieces will be needed:

4 posts, 1½ by 1½ by 28 in.
4 side rails, ¾ by 2 by 16 in.
4 end rails, ¾ by 2 by 7 in.
2 door rails, ¾ by 2 by 15 in.
2 door rails, ¾ by 2 by 22¾ in.
1 door panel, ¼ by 11½ by 19¼ in.
1 back panel, ¼ by 15½ by 23¼ in.
2 end panels, ¼ by 6½ by 23¼ in.
2 pieces for top and bottom, ½ by 6¾ by 15¾ in.

Square the four posts and bevel the tops as shown.

Cut grooves in them with a plow plane to receive the
¼-in. panels. The tenons on the rails are cut ¼ in.
wide and fit into the grooves in the posts the same
as the panels. The rails have grooves cut at the

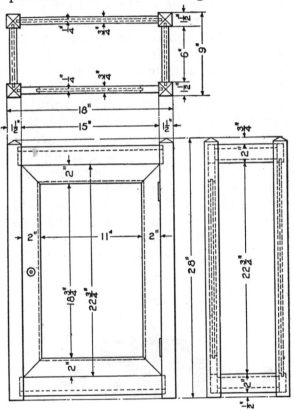

Details of Medicine Cabinet

inside edges for the panels. The front posts do not
have grooves on the inside but have two mortises,
one at each end for the top and bottom rails. The
back has a panel fitted in the same as the ends. See

that the pieces fit together perfecly square and
tight, then glue them together and give it time to
dry.

The top and bottom boards are next put in place.
The top is placed in the center of the top rails while
the bottom is put even with the lower edge of the
bottom rails, as shown in the detail drawing. The
door frame is mitered at the corners and rabbeted
on the inner edge to take the panel. A mirror can
be used in place of the panel if desired. Suitable
hinges and a catch, which can be purchased at a
hardware store, should be supplied for the door.

The shelves are of soft wood and are to be arranged to suit the maker. Before applying a finish,
go over the cabinet with fine sandpaper and remove
all the surplus glue about the joints and the rough
spots, else the finish will not take evenly. The finish
can be any one of the many different kinds supplied
by the trade for this purpose.

CONTENTS

MISSION FURNITURE

HOW TO MAKE IT

PART THREE

———

POPULAR MECHANICS HANDBOOKS

———

CHICAGO

POPULAR MECHANICS COMPANY

THIS book is one of the series of handbooks on industrial subjects being published by the Popular Mechanics Co. Like the magazine, these books are "written so you can understand it," and are intended to furnish information on mechanical subjects at a price within the reach of all.

The texts and illustrations have been prepared expressly for this Handbook Series, by experts; are up-to-date, and have been revised by the editor of Popular Mechanics.

THE dimensions given in the stock list contained in the description of each piece of furniture illustrated in this book call for material millplaned, sanded and cut to length. If the workman desires to have a complete home-made article, allowance must be made in the dimensions for planing and squaring the pieces. S-4-S and S-2-S are abbreviations for surface four sides and surface two sides.

A PIANO BENCH

The piano bench shown in the accompanying picture was made of black walnut and was finished natural. The finish was applied in the following manner: First, all the parts were well scraped and sandpapered, then the surface was covered with a coating of boiled linseed oil. After this had stood

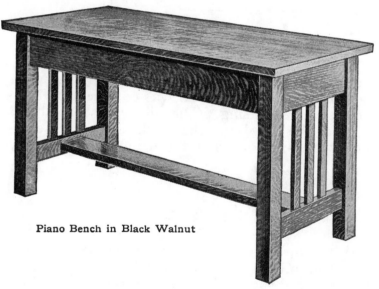

Piano Bench in Black Walnut

several hours, or until it had had time to penetrate the wood, the surplus liquid was wiped off with a flannel cloth. After the oil had stood for 48 hours, a thin coat of shellac was applied and allowed to harden overnight. The next morning this shellac was sandpapered lightly with No. 00 paper and a coat of floor wax was applied according to the directions which are found upon every can. Two

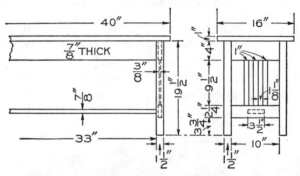

Detail of the Piano Bench

more coats of wax were applied after intervals of half an hour and the finish was completed. The effect is very pleasing. The oil brings out the rich color of the wood and the shellac and wax serve to preserve the color. The following stock is needed:

1 top, 1 by 16½ by 40½ in., S-2-S.
4 posts, 1½ by 1½ by 20 in., S-4-S.
2 rails, ⅞ by 4¼ by 36 in., S-2-S.
2 rails, ⅞ by 4¼ by 13 in., S-2-S.
2 lower rails, ⅞ by 2½ by 13 in., S-2-S.
1 stretcher, ⅞ by 3¾ by 36 in., S-2-S.
6 slats, ⅜ by 1¼ by 11 in., S-2-S.

With the exception of the legs all the stock is specified mill-planed to thickness upon two surfaces. The legs are specified planed on four sides. Square the legs to length and the rails, stretcher, slats, etc., to width and length.

Lay out and work the tenons of the rails and stretcher. The slats are best made without tenons, the whole end of each slat being "housed" into the rails. The reason for this is obvious—it is a difficult matter to fit two or more pieces between fixed parts when their ends are tenoned. When the ends are housed any slight variation in the lengths adjusts itself. It is necessary, however, to chisel the sides of the mortises carefully, but this is a simple matter compared with getting the shoulders of the tenons, etc., all just alike.

Assemble the parts, using good hot glue. Put the ends of the bench together first. When the glue has hardened on these, place the stretcher and side rails. Fasten the top to the frame from the under side, either by glued blocks and screws or by angle irons.

A LIBRARY TABLE

A library table of neat appearance and correct proportions is shown in the accompanying sketch and detail drawing. This table looks best when finished in quarter-sawed oak, although any of the other furniture woods can be used if desired. If the material is ordered from the mill cut to length, squared and sanded, much of the hard labor can be avoided. Order the following pieces:

4 legs, 2 by 2 by 30¼ in., S-4-S.
1 top, 1⅛ by 30 by 42 in., S-4-S.
2 end pieces, ¾ by 17⅛ by 29 in., S-2-S.
2 top rails, ⅞ by 2 by 37 in., S-4-S.
2 top rails, ⅞ by 2 by 25½ in., S-4-S.
1 lower brace, ¾ by 2 by 32 in., S-4-S.
4 shelves, ¾ by 7 by 29 in., S-4-S.
8 slats, ¼ by 1⅛ by 17⅛ in., S-4-S.
2 drawer fronts, ¾ by 5¾ by 25 in., S-4-S.
4 drawer sides, ⅜ by 3¾ by 14 in., soft wood.
2 drawer ends, ⅜ by 3⅜ by 24¼ in., soft wood.
2 drawer bottoms, ⅜ by 13¼ by 24¼ in., soft wood.
2 drawer supports, ¾ by 2 by 23½ in., soft wood.
2 drawer supports, ¾ by 2 by 25 in., soft wood.

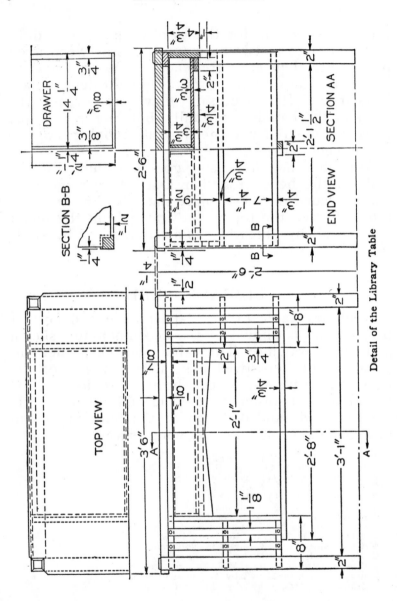

Detail of the Library Table

Start work on the legs by beveling the tops and squaring them up and laying out the mortises for the shelves as shown in section BB. Care should be taken to get the legs mortised in pairs and all cut the same height. This is best done by placing the four legs side by side with the ends square, and then laying out the mortises across all four at once with a try-square.

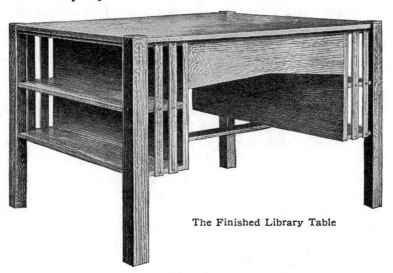

The Finished Library Table

The table top is made of several boards which are doweled and glued together. Be careful to get the best side of each board up and have the joints a tight fit. The corners should be cut out for the posts as shown. The posts are to be fastened to the board by means of screws. The holes can be counterbored for the heads and then plugged. The top rails are also fastened to the top board by means of screws.

The end pieces can now be made. Two or more

boards will have to be glued together for these. The top corners will have to be cut to fit about the top rails. Cleats can be used in fastening them to the top board. The shelves also have the corners cut to fit into the mortises in the posts. They are held to the end boards by means of screws.

If the parts all fit perfectly square and tight, they can be glued and screwed together, which will complete the table except for the slats and drawers. The slats can be fastened on with nails, then the heads covered with fancy nails which can be secured for this purpose. The drawer supports can now-be put in. They are screwed to the end boards as shown. A bottom brace should be fastened under the lower shelves to help steady the table. The two drawers are made as shown in the detail sketch. No handles are needed as the lower edge of the front board can be used for pulling them out.

When the table is complete it should be carefully gone over with fine sandpaper and all rough spots removed. Scrape the glue from about the joints as finish will not take where there is any glue. Apply the stain preferred or the one that matches the other furniture. This can be any of the many stains supplied by the trade for this purpose.

A PRINCESS DRESSER

A design of a princess dresser that is well proportioned and of pleasing appearance is shown in the accompanying sketch and detail drawing. The cost is very moderate and if a mill is not too far away, a great amount of labor can be saved by ordering

Dresser Made of Quarter-Sawed Oak

the material ready cut to length, squared and sanded. Quarter-sawed oak should be used and the material needed will be as follows:

    4 posts, 1¾ by 1¾ by 27 in., S-4-S.
    1 top board, ¾ by 17 by 37 in., S-2-S.
    5 side rails, ¾ by 1½ by 37½ in., S-4-S.
    4 end rails, ¾ by 2 by 17½ in., S-4-S.
    2 end panels, ¼ by 16¼ by 16¾ in., S-4-S.
    1 drawer partition, 1 by 7¾ by 18½ in., S-4-S.
    1 back board, ¾ by 4½ by 36 in., S-2-S.
    2 mirror supports, ⅞ by 2½ by 30 in., S-4-S.
    2 side pieces for mirror, ¾ by 2 by 42 in., S-4-S.
    2 end pieces for mirror, ¾ by 2 by 21½ in., S-4-S.
    2 drawer fronts, ¾ by 7 by 17½ in., S-4-S.
    1 drawer front, ¾ by 7 by 36 in., S-4-S.
    1 20 by 38 bevel mirror.

The following pieces may be of any soft wood:

    5 drawer slides, ¾ by 2 by 17 in.
    6 drawer sides, ½ by 7 by 17 in.
    2 drawer bottoms, ½ by 17 by 17 in.
    1 drawer bottom, ½ by 17 by 35½ in.
    4½ sq. ft. of ⅜-in. pine for back.

First be sure the posts are perfectly square and of equal length. Either chamfer or round the upper ends as desired. The mortises can now be laid out and cut or they can be left until the rail tenons are all made and then marked and cut directly from each tenon. The posts as well as the end rails should have grooves cut in them to take the ¼-in. end panels.

The top board should have the corners cut to fit about the posts. The corners of the back board should be rounded as shown in the drawing.

The end sections of the dresser can be glued together first, care being taken to get the joints square and tight. When these are dry the side rails and drawer slides can be fitted and glued in place. The top board is held in position by means of screws through cleats which are fastened to the inner sides of the rails.

The mirror frame is made by mortising the end

pieces with the side pieces as shown. It is rabbeted on the back to hold a 20 by 38-in. mirror.
After the mirror is securely fastened in the frame

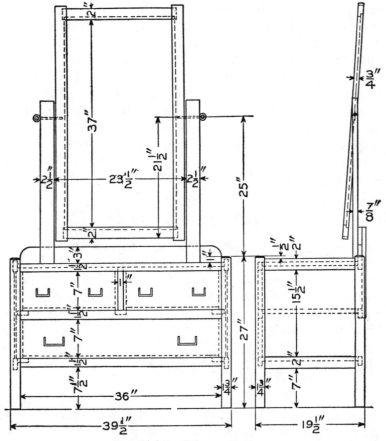

Detail of the Princess Dresser

a thin wood covering should be tacked on the back
to protect the glass. The frame swings between

two upright posts which are securely fastened to the body of the dresser as shown.

The drawers are made and fitted in the usual manner. The drawing shows two drawers in the top compartment, but one exactly like the lower can be made and used instead by simply leaving out the 1 in. partition. Suitable handles for the drawers can be purchased at any hardware store.

The back is made of soft wood and is put on in the usual manner. Scrape all surplus glue from about the joints as the stain will not take where there is any glue. Finish smooth with fine sandpaper and apply the stain desired, which may be any of the many mission stains supplied by the trade for this purpose.

A SEWING BOX

A rather unique sewing box, and one that is quite as convenient as unique, is shown in the illustration. The material is walnut and ash. The posts are walnut and the slats and top rail ash. Both are finished in their natural colors. The following is the stock bill:

    4 posts, 1½ in. in diameter and 15 in. long, walnut.
    1 bottom, ⅜ by 16½ by 16½ in., S-2-S, walnut.
    4 top rails, ⅜ by 1½ by 20 in., S-2-S, ash.
    4 under rails, ⅝ by ¾ by 20 in., S-2-S, walnut.
    72 slats, ⅛ by ⅝ by 6½ in., S-2-S, ash.

In ordering the stock it will be wise to combine the lengths of pieces having like widths and thicknesses.

If not possible to secure doweling of the diameter indicated for the verticals, it is an easy matter to

take a square piece of stock, lay it off and work it
into an eight-sided prism. After this, the arrises
may again be planed until it has 16 and then 32
sides. The rest may be removed with sandpaper.
Or it is possible that curtain pole stock will be

Sewing Box Made of
Walnut and Ash

available. Saw these posts to length and leave the
ends square.

Square up the stock for the other parts. Work
the bottom piece to a 16-in. square. The rails are
not to be squared on the ends but are to be mitered
each in turn. The bottom is fastened to the posts
by metal brackets.

Chisel out recesses in the posts so that the bottom may be inserted. Insert the corners and use

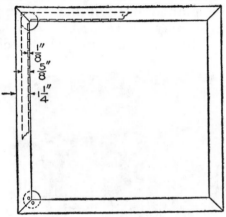

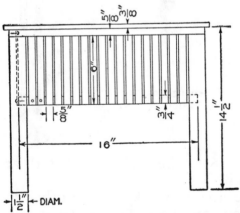

Detail of the Sewing Box

glue and nails to hold them in place. Place the lower of the two top rails, notching out the posts as is necessary to bring the inner edge of these rails in position. Fasten to the posts. Miter and place the top rails. The slats, it will be noted, are fastened to the bottom from the outer side and to the lower of the two top rails from the inner side. Brassheaded tacks such as upholsterers use are required.

In finishing, sandpaper all parts and then apply a coat of boiled linseed oil. Allow this to stand a half hour or so and then wipe the surface clean. After this has dried thoroughly apply a thin coating of shellac and allow it to harden. Sand the shellac when hard with No. 00 sandpaper and then apply several coats of wax, polishing in the usual manner.

Two pairs of castors will add to the ease with which the box may be moved about.

A FERN STAND

When making the fern stand shown in the accompanying sketch use quarter-sawed oak if possible, as this wood is the most suitable for finishing in the different mission stains. Considerable labor can be saved in its construction by ordering the stock from the mill ready cut to length, squared and sanded. Order the following pieces:

    4 posts, 1½ by 1½ by 30 in., S-4-S.
    8 side rails, ¾ by 1½ by 13½ in., S-4-S.
    2 shelf supports, ¾ by 1 by 13½ in., S-4-S.
    1 top, ¾ by 16 by 16 in., S-4-S.
    1 shelf, ¾ by 15 by 15 in., S-4-S.
    16 slats, ⅜ by 3 by 5 in., S-4-S.

The legs are made first. Be sure they are square and of equal length. The mortises can be laid out and cut or they can be left until the tenons on the side rails are all made, then marked and cut from

each tenon. The top rails and the slats are exactly
alike for the four sides, as the table is square. In
addition to the tenons on the rails, grooves should
be cut in each for the ends of the slats to fit into
as shown in the cross section in the detail drawing.
Holes should be cut in the slats as shown.

The top board should have the corners cut out
to fit around the posts. It is held in place by means

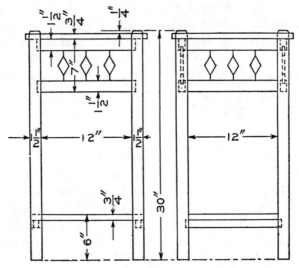

Detail of the Fern Stand

of screws through cleats which are fastened to the
inner sides of the top rails.

The bottom board or shelf rests upon two rails
that are mortised into the posts as shown. The top
and bottom boards should be of one piece if possible,
otherwise two or more boards will have to be glued
together.

Before gluing up the joints see that all the pieces

fit together square and tight. The posts and rails should be glued and assembled, then the top and bottom boards put in place to hold the frame square when the clamps are put on.

Finished Stand in Quartered Oak

Leave to dry for about 24 hours before removing the clamps. Fasten the top and bottom boards in place and then go over the stand with fine sandpaper and remove all surplus glue and rough spots.

A WARDROBE

The wardrobe or clothes closet shown in the accompanying sketch and detail drawing will be found a great convenience in a bedroom where closet space is limited or where there is no closet at all. It provides ample room for hanging suits, dresses and other wearing apparel, as well as space for boots and shoes. It can be made of any of the several furniture woods in common use, but quarter-sawed oak will be found to give the most pleasing effect. The stock should be ordered from the mill ready cut to length, squared and sanded. In this way much labor will be saved. The following pieces will be needed:

4 posts, 1¾ by 1¾ by 64½ in., S-4-S.
2 front rails, ¾ by 1½ by 37½ in., S-4-S.
1 top and 1 bottom board, each ¾ by 18½ by 37 in., S-4-S.
1 top back rail, ¾ by 4¼ by 37½ in., S-4-S.
1 lower back rail, ¾ by 4 by 37½ in., S-4-S.
6 end rails, ¾ by 6 by 18½ in., S-4-S.
4 end uprights, ¾ by 4 by 22½ in., S-4-S.
8 end panels, ⅜ by 7½ by 22½ in., S-4-S.
5 shelves, ¾ by 17¾ by 19½ in., S-4-S.
2 drawer fronts, ¾ by 4¾ by 8½ in., S-4-S.
1 door, ¾ by 7¾ by 10 in., S-4-S.
1 shelf partition, ¾ by 10 by 19 in., S-4-S.
2 drawer fronts, ¾ by 7 by 17 in., S-4-S.
1 drawer front, ¾ by 8 by 17 in., S-4-S.
1 partition (several pieces), ¾ by 19½ by 57¾ in., S-4-S.
4 door uprights, ¾ by 2½ by 57 in., S-4-S.
2 top rails, ¾ by 3½ by 14½ in., S-4-S.
2 middle rails, ¾ by 6 by 14½ in., S-4-S.
2 lower rails, ¾ by 4½ by 14½ in., S-4-S.
4 center uprights, ¾ by 2½ by 23 in., S-4-S.
8 panels, ⅜ by 6 by 22½ in., S-4-S.
4 pieces, ⅜ by 4¾ by 19 in., soft wood.
2 pieces, ⅜ by 8 by 19 in., soft wood.
2 pieces, ⅜ by 4¼ by 8 in., soft wood.
4 pieces, ½ by 7 by 19 in., soft wood.
3 pieces, ½ by 16½ by 19 in., soft wood.
2 pieces, ½ by 6½ by 16½ in., soft wood.
2 pieces, ½ by 8 by 19 in., soft wood.
1 piece, ½ by 7½ by 16½ in., soft wood.
1 back (several pieces), ⅜ by 36 by 58 in., S-2-S.

The Wardrobe Complete

First be sure the posts are perfectly square and of equal length. The upper ends can be chamfered or rounded if desired. The two front posts are alike, as are the back ones. The mortises should be laid out in each pair of posts and then cut with a sharp chisel, or they can be left until the tenons are all made, and then marked and cut from each tenon. Grooves should be cut on one side of all the posts to take the end panels.

The front and lower back rails are plain except for the tenons at each end, but the end rails and the center uprights should have grooves cut for the panels the same as the posts. The top back rail serves as a top back board and should have the corners rounded as shown in the detail drawing.

The frame can now be assembled. Glue should be used on all the joints as it makes them much stiffer. Be careful to get the frame together perfectly square, or it will be hard to fit the doors and the shelves.

The top and bottom boards should have the corners cut to clear the posts. The closet is divided into two compartments by a partition. This can be made of plain boards or panels similar to those in the ends, as desired. Place the shelves in position as shown. They are held in place by means of cleats and screws. The one shelf has a partition in its center with a door on one side and two small drawers on the other. Drawers should be fitted to three of the other compartments. They are made in the usual manner except that the front boards should be cut out at the top for a handhold as shown.

The doors are fitted by a tenon and mortise joint

at the ends. They have a centerpiece and panels
to match the ends of the closet. Suitable hinges

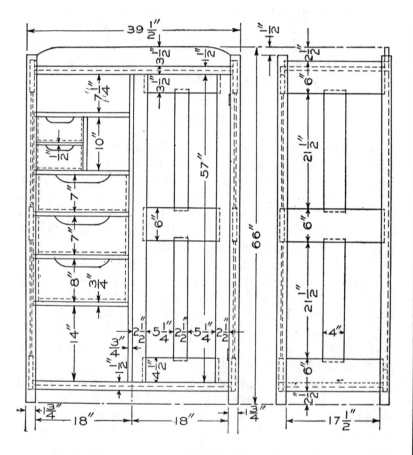

Detail of the Wardrobe

and a catch should be supplied. These can be purchased at any hardware store.

The backing is put on in the usual manner. It should be finished on the front side.

When complete, the closet should be carefully gone over with fine sandpaper and all glue and rough spots removed. Apply stain of the desired color. This may be any of the many mission stains supplied by the trade for this purpose.

A FINISH

An appropriate finish is obtained as follows: First thoroughly scrape and sandpaper the various parts, then apply a coat of brown Flemish water stain. Allow this to dry well, then sand it lightly with No. 00 sandpaper to lay the grain. Again apply the Flemish stain, but this time have it weakened by the addition of an equal amount of water. When dry, sand again as on the first coat. Upon the second coat of stain apply a thin coat of shellac. This is to protect the high lights from the stain in the filler which is to follow. Sand lightly, then apply a paste filler of a sufficiently dark shade to make a dark field for the brown Flemish. Clean off the surplus and polish in the usual manner.

Upon the filler, after it has hardened overnight, apply a coat of orange shellac. Successively apply several coats of some good rubbing varnish. Polish the first coats with haircloth or curled hair, and the last with pulverized pumice stone, mixed with raw linseed or crude oil.

AN OAK TABLE

The accompanying illustration shows another style of a mission table. The stock for this table if ordered as follows and sanded will require only the work of making the joints and putting them together:

4 posts, 2 in. square 30⅝ in., S-4-S.
4 upper rails, ⅞ by 6½ by 22½ in., S-2-S.
2 lower rails, ⅞ by 3 by 22½ in., S-2-S.
2 top pieces, ⅞ by 12½ by 24½ in., S-2-S.
6 slats, ⅜ by 3½ by 15½ in., S-2-S.
1 stretcher, ⅞ by 8½ by 21½ in., S-2-S.

This table may be made with mortise and tenon joints or with dowels as desired. If dowels are used, the upper and lower rails should be made 2 in. shorter than shown in the drawing.

Be sure to get the pieces for the posts with their surfaces square to each other and their ends sawed square off. This will simplify the assembling a great deal. Make the posts exactly the same length, 30½ in., and chamfer a ⅜-in. bevel on their tops.

Square up the four upper rails, 6 by 22 in., marking the working face and edge to work from when laying out the tenons later. Square up the two lower rails, 2½ by 22 in. These must be exactly the same length as the upper rails. The two ends of the table having the slats should be glued up first. Lay out the tenons on the upper and lower rails for these two ends and be sure to work from the marked face and edges, using a knife line. Cut the tenons, and, by placing them against the posts in the exact position they are to occupy, mark the places for the mortises. These joints should be numbered so that each mortise may be cut to fit its own tenon.

Square up the slats, 3 by 15⅛ in., and cut mortises

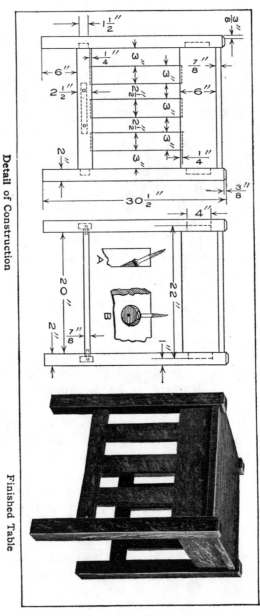

Detail of Construction

Finished Table

in the upper and lower rails ¼ in. deep to let them in. The number of these slats, their size and spacing may be arranged to suit one's own idea. Put the posts, upper and lower rails, and slats together without glue first to determine if the parts fit properly, and then glue and clamp them together. Hot glue will hold best, if the room and lumber are warm; if not, it is best to use ordinary liquid glue. While the glue on these two ends of the table is setting, the other upper rails, top, and stretcher may be finished.

The top will have to be made of two or three pieces joined together with dowels and glue. If possible, use only two boards and be sure the grain in both pieces runs the same way when they are put together.

After the ends which were glued have set at least 24 hours, the clamps may be taken off and the other two upper rails tenoned and mortised in place. The stretcher may be held with two ⅜-in. dowels in each end, or with two round-head screws put through the lower rails. When gluing up the whole table, be sure the sides are square to each other. The top may now be squared up 24 by 24 in. and the corners cut out for the top of the posts. The top may be fastened as shown at A and B in the drawing, or by cleats screwed to the inside of the upper rails and top.

Before staining, be sure that all surplus glue is scraped off and the surfaces sanded clean. A weathered or fumed oak stain is suitable for this table. A good weathered oak stain may be made by mixing a little drop black ground in oil with turpentine and a little linseed oil. Put this stain on with a brush and allow to stand until it begins to flatten or dull, then rub off across the grain with a rag or piece of cotton waste. When thoroughly dry, apply one coat of very thin shellac. After this has dried, finish with two coats of wax. The shellac prevents the turpentine in the wax from rubbing out the stain. To get a good wax finish the work should dry until it will not show finger marks, before rubbing.

BOOK TROUGH

A very cheap but attractive book trough is shown in the accompanying photograph. This piece of

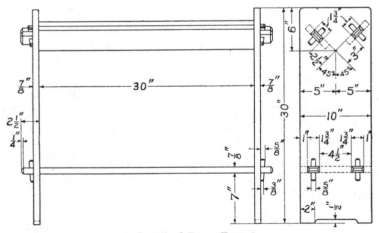

Detail of Book Trough

mission furniture will be found useful in the home or office and can be made by anyone who has a slight knowledge of tools. The material should be either oak or chestnut, which can be secured from the planing mill dressed and sandpapered ready to cut the tenons and mortises. The stock needed will be as follows:

2 ends, ⅞ in. by 10 in. by 31 in., S-2-S.
1 shelf, ⅞ in. bv 10 in. by 35 in., S-1-S.
2 trough pieces, ⅞ in. by 4 in. by 35 in., S-2-S.
8 keys, ⅝ in. by ⅝ in. by 3 in.

The two end pieces should be made first with the

Book Trough Complete

top corners rounded off and the lower end, which is of simple design, can be cut out with a bracket saw and smoothed with a wood rasp. The mortises should then be laid out according to the sketch and cut, by first boring ¾-in. holes and finishing with a chisel, being careful to keep all edges clean and free from slivers.

The shelf can now be made by cutting a double-key tenon at each end to fit the end pieces. The space between the two tenons at each end can be cut out with a bracket saw and finished with a rasp. The key holes should be mortised as shown in the sketch. The trough pieces are made in a similar manner, care being taken to have all tenons and mortises perfectly square and a good fit, so the trough when assembled will have a neat and workmanlike appearance. The trough can be finished in any one of the many mission finishes which are supplied by the trade for this purpose.

AN OAK SERVING TABLE

The serving table is another useful piece of furniture that can be made in mission style. This table should be made in quarter-sawed oak and stained very light. The stock order is as follows:

    2 posts, 2 by 2 by 37 in., S-4-S.
    2 posts, 2 by 2 by 31 in., S-4-S.
    1 top, 1 by 21 by 40 in., S-2-S.
    2 side rails, ¾ by 3 by 34½ in., S-2-S.
    4 end rails, ¾ by 3 by 15½ in., S-2-S.
    1 back panel, ¾ by 4 by 34½ in., S-2-S.
    1 stretcher, 1 by 5 by 36½ in., S-4-S.
    1 slat, ½ by 1½ by 36 in., S-4-S.

The four posts are ordered 1 in. longer than necessary for squaring to length and the two back posts should be chamfered ¼ in. on top, as they are the longest and project above the back panel. All of the posts are cut tapering for a space of 4 in. from the bottom ends. Mortises in the posts and tenons on the rails are laid out and cut as shown by the dimensions in the drawing. These parts are then well glued and put together. The top, which should be of well sea-

Serving Table Complete

soned wood, is cut to fit around the back posts so the back edge and the back side of the posts are flush. The back panel is placed in mortises cut in the corners of the back posts. This is done so the back surface of the panel will be flush the same as the edge of the top. The slat is fastened with round-headed brass screws on the front of the two back posts about half way between the top and the ends of the posts.

The top may be fastened to the rails by one of two methods. One way is to use a small button made of wood and so mortised as to set in the rails and then

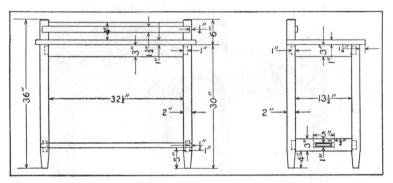

Detail of Serving Table

fastened to the top with screws. About six of these buttons will be sufficient to hold the top in place. The other method is to bore a hole slanting on the inside of the rails, directing the bit toward the top, which will make a seat—if not cut too deep—for a screw that can be turned direct into the top.

The glue must be removed from about the joints and the surfaces smoothed over with fine sandpaper before applying the stain. The directions for staining will be found on the can in which it is sold. The grain of the wood will show up well if the surface is given a dull waxed finish after staining.

AN UMBRELLA STAND

The umbrella stand shown in the accompanying illustration will be found quite appropriate for the hall or reception room that is furnished in mission style. It can be made of any of the furniture woods, but quarter-sawed oak gives the best results. The stock necessary to make this stand can be secured from the mill ready cut to length, squared and sanded, and is given in the following list:

4 posts, 1½ by 1½ by 28 in., S-4-S.
4 top rails, ⅞ by 2 by 10 in., S-2-S.
4 lower rails, ⅞ by 3 by 10 in., S-2-S.
4 slats, ⅜ by 3 by 20 in., S-2-S.
1 bottom, ⅞ by 10 by 10 in.

First square up the posts and bevel the tops as shown in the detail sketch. Place them side by side, on a flat surface with the ends square and lay out the mortises with a try-square on all four pieces at the same time. This will insure your getting them all straight and of the same height. Now lay out the tenons on the rails in the same manner and cut them to fit the mortises in the posts. Mortises should also be cut in the rails for the ends of the side slats as shown. Try all the joints and see that they fit tight and square. Glue two sides of the stand together and let them dry for at least 24 hours, then glue the remaining parts, being careful to get everything together perfectly square.

The bottom board can now be fitted in place. It

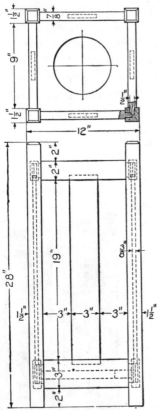

should have a hole cut in it for the drip pan. The pan should be about 6 or 7 in. in diameter. One suitable for the purpose can be purchased in any hardware store. The bottom board can be fastened to the rails with nails driven from the under side, or cleats can be nailed to the rails for it to rest upon.

When the stand is complete, scrape all glue from about the joints and go over the whole with fine sandpaper, removing all rough spots. Apply the finish you like best, or the one that will match your other furniture.

Should the builder want an entire hand-made stand, the drip pan may be beaten into shape from sheet brass or copper. This kind of work is known as repoussé. After beating the pan into shape, it can be finished in antique, old copper or given a polished surface, as desired.

A CHAFING-DISH BUFFET

The chafing-dish buffet is something very convenient and attractive for the dining room. For the

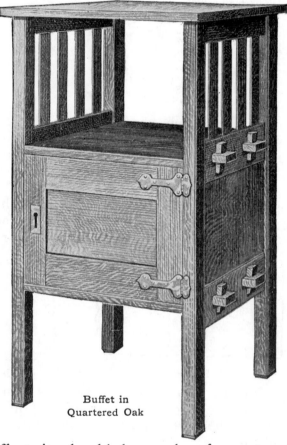

**Buffet in
Quartered Oak**

best effect it should be made of quartered oak, stained brown or weathered and trimmed with brass hardware.

To save a great deal of uninteresting labor, secure the following pieces of stock, surfaced on four sides and cut to length:

4 legs, 1½ by 1½ by 36 in., S-4-S.
4 rails, ⅞ by 4 by 10 in., S-4-S.
2 rails, ⅞ by 3 by 10 in., S-4-S.
2 panels, ⅜ by 9⅜ by 9½ in., S-4-S.
1 panel, ⅜ by 6½ by 9½ in., S-4-S.
2 shelves, ⅞ by 12 by 19 in., S-4-S.
1 top, ⅞ by 16 by 20 in., S-4-S.
2 stiles for door, ⅞ by 2 by 12 in., S-4-S.
2 rails for door, ⅞ by 3 by 10 in., S-4-S.
1 back, ⅞ by 12 by 13 in., S-4-S.
8 slats, ⅜ by 1 by 8 in., S-4-S.

Begin the work on the rails for the sides of the stand. Have them all squared up to exactly the same length and to the correct width and thickness. Mark the tenons on the ends of each and cut them with a saw and chisel.

When this is finished, try the legs to see that they are all the same length and that their surfaces are square with each other. Next mark the mortises in

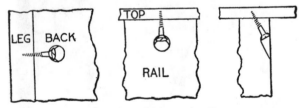

Method of Fastening with Screws

the legs for the tenons of the rails. To make the mortises, first bore to depth with a bit ⅛ in. smaller than the width of the mortise and cut to the line with a chisel.

Before gluing up the sides, cut the mortises in two lower rails for the tenons on the ends of the shelves. These tenons, with the smaller mor-

tises in them for the keys, should be cut first.
Square up the two side panels and cut grooves ⅜
in. wide and ¼ in. deep for them in the rails and
part of the legs.

Make the eight slats 8 in. long, 1 in. wide and

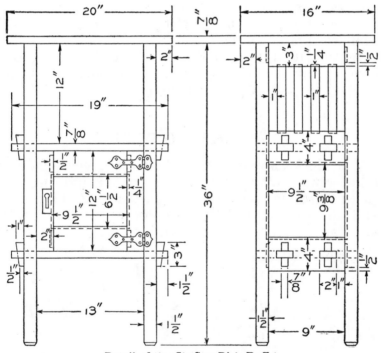

Detail of the Chafing-Dish Buffet

⅜ in. thick, and cut mortises for them in the two
upper rails.

The two sides of the buffet are now ready to
be glued up and clamped. While the glue on these
is setting, make the door. The rails are mortised

into the stiles ½ in. and both are grooved to receive the panel. It is best to get the stock a little full for the door so that it may be made up a little larger than necessary and planed down to fit.

There only remains to fit in the shelves and fasten the top and back. The top and back are held with screws as shown in sketch.

Taper the keys only slightly, otherwise they will keep working loose.

Stain with two coats of weathered oak, give one coat of thin shellac to fix the stain and two coats of wax for a soft-gloss finish.

A WRITING DESK

The desk shown in the illustration was made of plain-sawed white oak. The copper lighting fixtures were made by the amateur as were the hinges and the drawer pulls. The doors are fitted with art-glass panels. The following stock list is needed:

1 top, ¾ by 22½ by 41 in., S-2-S.
4 posts, 2 by 2 by 31 in., S-4-S.
2 rails, ¾ by 6¼ by 19 in., S-2-S.
2 rails, ¾ by 6¼ by 35 in., S-2-S.
2 rails, ¾ by 3¼ by 19 in., S-2-S.
1 stretcher, ¾ by 3¼ by 35 in., S-2-S.
2 drawer fronts, ¾ by 4¼ by 14 in., S-2-S.
4 drawer sides, ½ by 4¼ by 19 in., S-2-S.
2 drawer backs, ⅜ by 4 by 14 in., S-2-S.
2 drawer bottoms, ⅜ by 19 by 14 in., S-2-S.
4 slides, ¾ by 2½ by 19 in., S-2-S.
8 guides, ¾ by 2 by 10 in., S-2-S.
2 cabinet posts, 1 by 1 by 16 in., S-4-S.
4 cabinet posts, 1 by 1 by 11 in., S-4-S.
1 back, ¾ by 16 by 35 in., S-2-S.
1 shelf, ¾ by 8 by 35 in., S-2-S.
2 shelves, ¾ by 8 by 15 in., S-2-S.
4 door pieces, ⅝ by 1 by 15 in., S-2-S.
8 door pieces, ⅝ by 1 by 4 in., S-2-S.

Square the legs to length and lay out and cut the

mortises thereon. Lay off the tenons on the rails, after having squared the rails to length and width, and cut them.

Work up the top of the table and then the drawer stock and cabinet. Assemble the ends of the frame first, using good hot glue and enough clamps to

Writing Desk Made of Plain-Sawed Oak

hold the parts together properly. After the glue has hardened on these, the clamps may be removed and the front, back rails and the stretcher assembled.

While the glue is hardening on the main frame

the top cabinet may be built and assembled. This cabinet is detachable from the table proper and is to be held in place by means of cleats upon the back. These cleats are not specified in the bill; they may be obtained from scrap stock.

For a piece of woodwork of this style some of the softer browns of the mission stains will be most appropriate. After all parts have been thoroughly

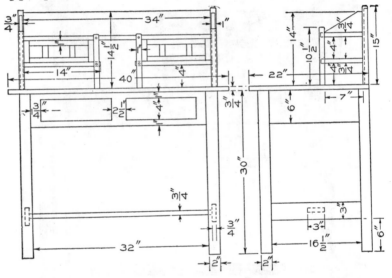

Detail of the Writing Desk

cleaned by scraping and sandpapering, a stain may be applied. Allow this to dry, then sand it lightly and apply a thin coat of shellac. Sand the shellac lightly and apply a filler of a color to match the stain, but darker in tone, of course. Clean off the surplus in the usual manner and then apply a coat of shellac. Sand this lightly and apply several coats of some good polishing wax.

MUSIC RACK AND BOOKSTAND

The illustration shows a very handy music and bookstand, which also can be used at the bedside as a reading stand. The following list of material will be required for construction:

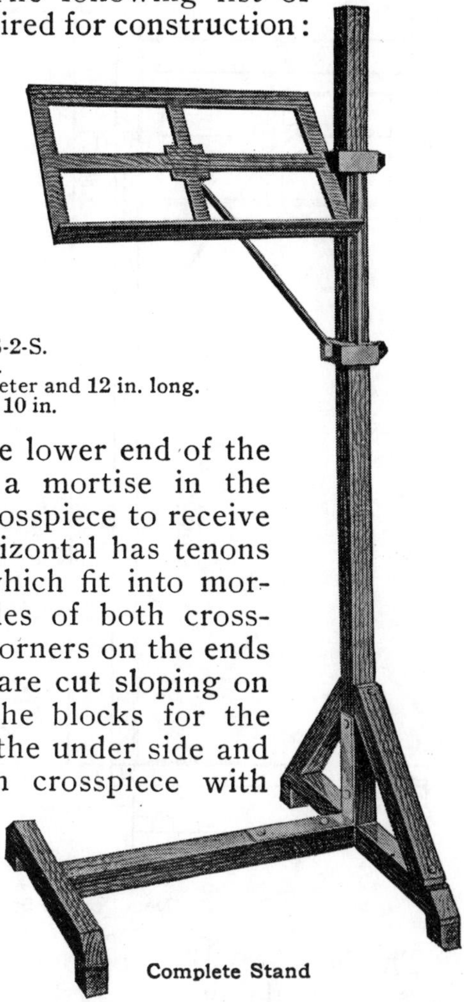

1 standard, 1⅛ by 1⅛ by 37 in., S-4-S.
1 horizontal, 1⅛ by 1⅛ by 15 in., S-4-S.
1 crosspiece, 1⅛ by 1⅛ by 14 in., S-4-S.
1 crosspiece, 1⅛ by 1⅛ by 12 in., S-4-S.
2 braces, 1⅛ by 1⅛ by 9 in., S-4-S.
1 board, ½ by 8 by 13 in., S-2-S.
4 blocks, 1⅛ in. square.
2 gauge clamps.
1 strip, ½ by 1 by 13 in., S-2-S.
8 round-head brass screws.
1 brass rod, ¼ in. in diameter and 12 in. long.
1 brass piece, ¼ by ¾ by 10 in.

Cut a tenon on the lower end of the upright and make a mortise in the center of the long crosspiece to receive the tenon. The horizontal has tenons cut on both ends which fit into mortises cut in the sides of both crosspieces. The upper corners on the ends of both crosspieces are cut sloping on a 45-deg. angle. The blocks for the feet are attached to the under side and at the end on each crosspiece with screws and hot glue, the screw heads being sunk so that they will not catch on carpets or mar the floor.

Complete Stand

The braces are attached with round-head screws after they are cut on each end to fit the standard and crosspiece.

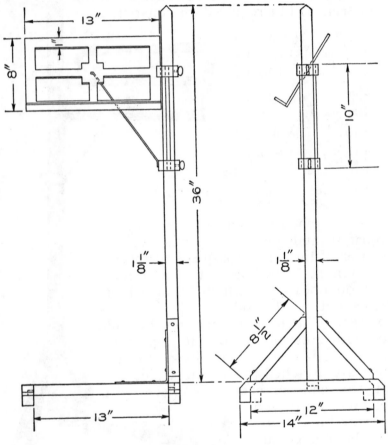

Detail of the Stand

The book rest is cut from the board. The openings are made by sawing the pieces out with a coping saw, and the edges are dressed up with a sharp chisel. The lip strip is then glued to the lower edge of the board.

One end of the board is now fitted into a slot cut in one of the gauge clamps. The slot must be cut at the right angle to give the desired slope to the book rest. The gauge clamps are joined with two small square strips of oak as shown. The small rod brace is flattened at both ends and a hole drilled in each to fasten it with screws as shown. The brass strip is bent in the middle at right angles and drilled to receive screws for fastening it in the corner of the upright and horizontal pieces.

A DICTIONARY AND MAGAZINE STAND

The accompanying picture shows a stand that is intended primarily for holding a large-size dictionary. The shelves may be utilized for holding books, magazines or sheet music. It will stand wear best if made of some hard wood, such as oak. Of the soft woods chestnut has the best grain for finishing, being hardly distinguishable from red oak.

The following pieces will be necessary:

```
2 sides, 3/4 by 16 by 38 1/2 in., S-4-S.
1 shelf, 3/4 by 15 1/2 by 21 in., S-2-S.
1 shelf, 3/4 by 14 by 17 in., S-2-S.
1 shelf, 3/4 by 13 1/2 by 21 in., S-2-S.
1 top, 3/4 by 13 by 17 in., S-2-S.
1 lip, 3/8 by 3/4 by 17 in., S-4-S.
8 keys, 3/4 by 1 by 3 1/2 in., S-2-S.
```

Begin work on the sides by preparing a joint edge on each piece and from this square up the lower ends and square lines across the inner surfaces to indicate the positions of the lower edges of the shelves.

Next, smooth off the mill marks from the broad surfaces of the shelves and square them to size on one edge and the two ends.

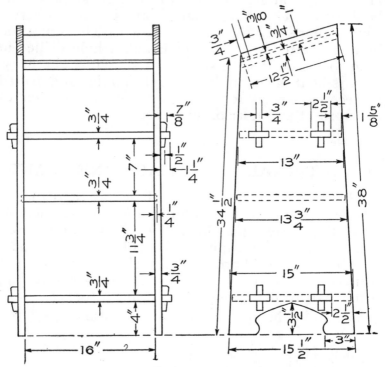

Detail of the Dictionary and Magazine Stand

Return to the side pieces and lay out the outline, but do not cut to these lines until the gains and mortises which are to receive the ends of the shelves and their tenons have been laid out and cut. Laying out these outlines at this time is done so as to

Stand Made in Oak

give the exact width the shelves are to have. These dimensions can be determined by measuring across the sides between the outlines at the points where the shelves are to be placed.

The shelves which have no tenons are to be let into the sides ¼ in. They should be shouldered ½ in. back from the edge so that the groove will not show on the face.

The lip on the front of the top shelf may be fastened by means of very small brads, the heads of which should be covered with putty, colored to match the finish.

A suitable finish may be obtained as follows:

First see that all the mill marks are removed, using a smooth plane and steel scraper and sandpaper, then apply a coat of cathedral-oak water stain. When dry, sandpaper lightly, using No. 00 paper. Apply a second coat of stain, diluting it by the addition of an equal volume of water. This is to produce a stronger contrast. Sand this lightly and put on a very thin coat of shellac to bind the filler and to prevent the stain in the filler which follows from discoloring the high lights. Sand this lightly and put on a coat of paste filler according to the directions that will be found on the can. This filler should be colored in the following proportions: Light paste filler, 20 lb.; Van Dyke brown, 1 lb. After the filler has hardened, sand it lightly and put on a coat of orange shellac. Follow this with several coats of some good rubbing varnish. The first coats should be rubbed with haircloth or curled hair, and the last with powdered pumice stone and raw linseed or crude oil.

A LEATHER BACK ARM CHAIR

A mission arm chair of simple design and construction is shown in the accompanying illustration. This chair is suitable for any room of the house

Arm Chair Complete

and can be made of wood to match other furniture.
Quarter-sawed oak is the wood most generally used,
and it is also very easy to obtain. The stock can be
ordered from the mill, cut to length, squared and

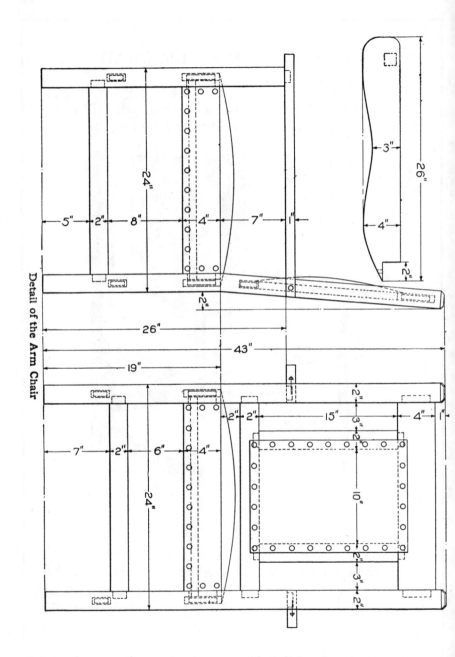

Detail of the Arm Chair

sanded. Following is a list of the material that will be needed:

2 front legs, 2 by 2 by 26¾ in.
2 back legs, 2 by 4 by 43 in.
2 arm rests, 1 by 4 by 26 in.
5 rails, ¾ by 4 by 21½ in.
5 rails, ¾ by 2 by 2½ in.
2 back pieces, ¾ by 2 by 16½ in.
1 piece leather, 31 in. square.
1 piece burlap, 28 in. square.
2 pieces leather, 13 by 18 in.
2 pieces burlap, 13 by 18 in.
1 box 8 oz. tacks.
5½ doz. ornamental nails.

Start with the front legs. Cut a tenon 1¼ in. square and ¾ in. long on one end to fit the arm rests. The mortises for the side rails are cut ½ in. wide and ⅞ in. deep. The tenons on the rails are cut to fit these mortises, care being taken to get them all the same length between shoulders. The back legs are cut with an offset of 2 in. as shown in the detail drawing and also have mortises cut in them for the back crosspieces. The upright pieces in the back are fastened into the crosspieces by means of tenons and mortises, and should be in place when the crosspieces are fastened to the legs.

The arms are cut from the 1 by 4 by 26-in. pieces. Be careful to get them so they will pair. The outside edge can be either curved or straight as desired. The front ends of the arms are held in place by mortises which fit over the tenons on the ends of the front legs, while the back ends are held in place by round-headed screws as shown.

The chair is now ready to be glued. Be sure to get the parts together perfectly square, and when dry scrape off all surplus glue around the joints, for stain will not adhere to glue and a white spot will be the result of failing to remove it. Go over the parts carefully with fine sandpaper and remove all rough marks. Then apply the stain you wish to use. To make the seat, first fit boards in the bottom and nail them to the side rails as shown. Fill the space with hair or elastic cotton felt to about 3 in. above the edge of the rails. Bind this down tightly with a piece of burlap and tack the edges to the rails. Cut out the corners of the burlap so that it will fit about the posts. Put the leather on over this and tack the edges to the bottoms of the rails. Then finish with the ornamental nails as shown.

To finish the back, first tack a piece of burlap over the opening, then place a layer of hair or cotton felt on this about 1 in. thick. Stretch the leather over this and fasten with ornamental nails. The back side is finished in the same manner, except that the hair is omitted.

A WALL SHELF

Coarse-grained woods make up into furniture and take a more satisfactory finish than close-grained woods. For this reason chestnut or oak is suggested for this shelf. Chestnut has a beautiful grain and is soft and easily worked.

There will be needed the following pieces:

Sides, 2 pieces, ¾ by 7¼ by 16½ in., S-2-S.
Lower shelf, 1 piece, ¾ by 6¼ by 30½ in., S-2-S.
Upper shelf, 1 piece, ¾ by 4¾ by 30½ in., S-2-S.
Lower back, 1 piece, ⅜ by 3½ by 30½ in., S-2-S.
Upper back, 1 piece, ⅜ by 3 by 30½ in., S-2-S.

In making out this stock bill the pieces have been specified ¼ in. wider and ½ in. longer than the finished piece is to be to allow for squaring up. The thicknesses are specified mill-planed exact so that all that is necessary is to merely plane off the mill-marks from the two broad surfaces.

It is quite possible that one may have a particular space or a particular set of books to place in the shelf. In such a case the length of the horizontals should be lengthened or shortened to meet the particular demands when ordering the lumber.

Begin work by squaring the horizontals to size. They are to be all of the same length. Next shape up the end pieces. The amount of slope for the front edges is indicated on the drawing. After all these pieces

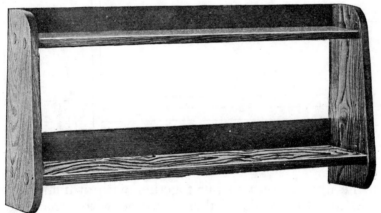

Complete Wall Shelf

have been squared up and the mill-marks removed, the dadoes or grooves and gains may be laid out and cut.

Beginners are prone to underestimate the importance of getting all the mill-marks off before putting on any finish. When boards are planed at the mill the planing is done by means of two or four knives revolving above or below the board—sometimes both above and below at the same time. These knives leave the surfaces filled with little ridges and hollows across the grain. These hollows, though they are hardly visible to the eye on the unfinished surface, show up as ugly streaks upon the surface after it has had a finish of stain and filler applied.

The joints here used are typical and the beginner can readily find how they are to be made from any good book on wood-working.

There are several ways of fastening the parts. They may be fastened by means of round-head blued screws. They may be fastened with carriage screws. The one

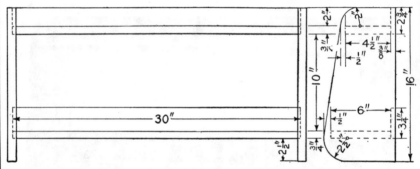

Wall Shelf Detail

in the illustration was put together with ordinary wire nails and the heads of these covered with ornamental heads to represent old-fashioned hand-wrought nails.

It will be found easier to apply the finish of stain and filler before the parts are assembled. A suitable finish is obtained as follows: After the parts are thoroughly sanded, put on a coat of Filipino water stain, wiping it off with an old cloth before it has had time to soak into the wood very much. Allow this to dry. Then sand lightly, using No. 00 paper, after which fill the pores of the wood with a black paste filler—directions will be found on the can. Follow this, when hardened, with several coats of floor wax.

A PEDESTAL

The pedestal shown in the accompanying illustration is another piece of furniture that can be made in the mission style. It is very simple in design and construction, and can be made by anyone who has a few simple tools and a slight knowledge of their use. It is best to make it of quarter-sawed oak as this is the most easily procured wood and also looks the best when finished. If you order the material from the mill ready cut to length, squared and sanded, much hard labor will be saved. Following is a list of the material needed:

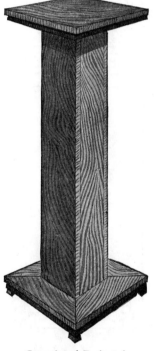

Completed Pedestal

1 top, ¾ by 12 by 12 in., S-1-S.
1 bottom, ¾ by 12 by 12 in., S-1-S
8 pieces, ¾ by 2 by 11 in.
2 sides, ¾ by 5 by 26 in., S-1-S.
2 sides, ¾ by 3½ by 26 in.
1 piece, ¾ by 6 by 6 in.
4 blocks, 1 in. square.

Having the boards for the post cut to the proper length and square, nail them together as shown in the detail drawing. Use finishing nails, then set the heads and fill the holes with putty. Next, nail the ¾ by 6-in. piece on one end of the post leaving the edges projecting even on all sides. Pick out the best board for the top. On the under side and ½ in. in from the edges, nail four

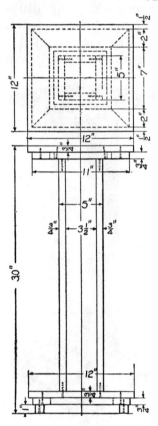

of the ¾ by 2 by 11-in. pieces which have been previously mitered as shown in the plan view. Now fasten this top to the post by nailing through the projecting edge of the top piece into the top board. Be careful to get this top on square with the post and exactly in center.

The bottom board is made in the same manner as the top board and is nailed to the lower end of the post as shown. Four 1-in. square blocks should be fastened to the bottom for the pedestal to rest on.

When complete, sandpaper smooth and apply any one of the many mission stains that are supplied by the trade for this purpose.

After staining the wood, the surface can be given a polished or dull finish, as desired. Mission furniture requires a dull finish, and this may be obtained by applying a coat of wax, well rubbed on the wood.

MAGAZINE RACK

The accompanying cut shows a magazine rack that will find favor with many amateur wood-workers on account of its simplicity in design and its rich, massive appearance when properly finished. It is so constructed that each piece may be polished, stained and finished before it is finally put together. Quarter-sawed oak is the best wood to use. Plain-sawed oak looks well, but it is more liable to warp than quarter-sawed and this is quite an element in pieces as wide as the ones here used. Following is a list of the material needed:

    4 posts, 2 by 2 by 40 in., S-4-S.
    5 shelves, 1 by 14 by 24 in., S-2-S.
    20 F.H. screws, 2 in. long.

Considerable labor can be saved if the material be ordered from the mill ready cut to length, squared and sanded. The corner posts should be made first. The most convenient and accurate method of laying out the mortises is to square one end of each post and lay them on the bench flat, with the squared ends even with each other; then clamp them securely and lay out the mortises on one side across all four pieces at once; then loosen the clamp and project the marks to the other side with a try-square. Now saw along these marks, making each cut just deep enough to bring the mortises diagonally across the piece from one corner to the opposite corner as shown in the detail sketch. Be careful not to get the mortises wider than the shelves are thick. Bevel the tops of the posts as shown.

See that the ends of the shelves are square and smooth, then set a scratch gauge so that the scriber is just 2 in. from the face of the block and mark this

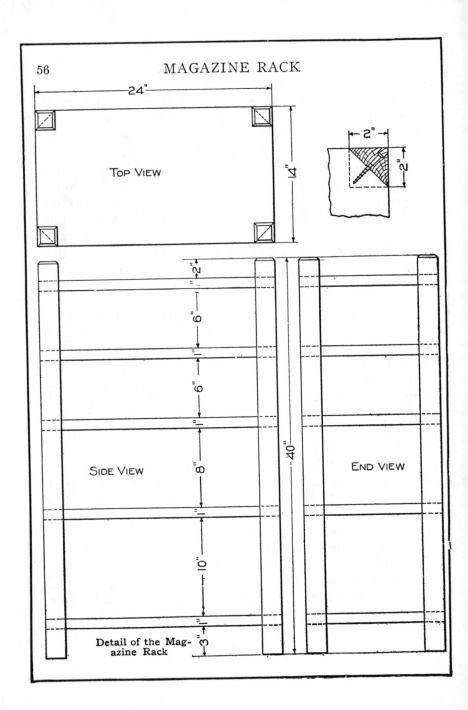

MAGAZINE RACK

24"

TOP VIEW

14"

2"

2"

2"

6"

6"

40"

8"

SIDE VIEW

END VIEW

10"

Detail of the Magazine Rack

3"

Magazine Rack Complete

αistance off each way from the corner of the shelves. Saw these corners diagonally across as shown, being careful not to saw off too much.

The parts can now be assembled. Place all the parts in position, then pass a rope around each end and twist it up tightly with a small stick. If this is properly done, you can now pick up the rack and handle it in any way you wish. The screws can now be put in the corners. You can use flat-head screws and plug the holes, or you can use round-head blue screws and let the heads project. After the screws are all in, dress off all unevenness where the shelves are mortised into the posts, then mark each shelf and post so that you can put it together again after the parts are finished. Take the rack apart and transfer the marks to some part of the mortises and shelves that will not be covered with the finish you intend to put on. Apply the finish you wish to use and when the parts are thoroughly dry they can be reassembled and your rack will be complete.

A HALL TREE

When making the hall tree as shown in the accompanying illustration use quarter-sawed oak if possible, as this wood is the most suitable for finishing in the different mission stains. This is a very useful and attractive piece of mission furniture and is also very easy to construct. The stock can be purchased ready cut to length, mill-planed and sandpapered on four sides as given in the following list:

1 post, 2 by 2 by 59 in.
4 posts, 2 by 2 by 10 in.
8 braces, ⅞ by 2 by 7½ in.
4 arms, ⅞ by 2 by 5¾ in.

First square up all the posts and bevel them at the tops as shown. Then cut the mortises making them

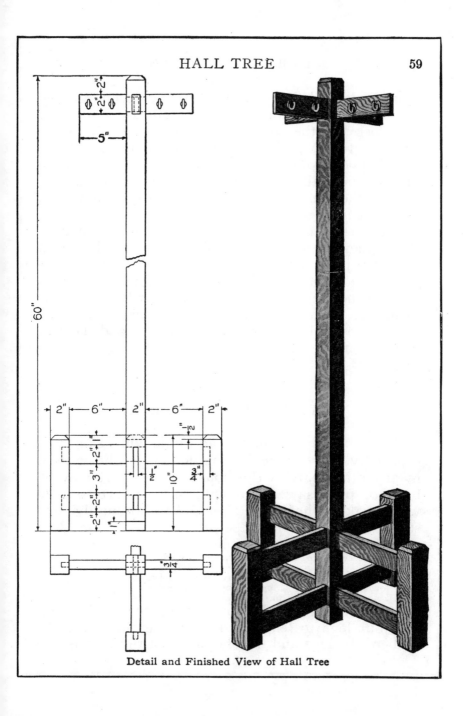

Detail and Finished View of Hall Tree

½ in. wide and ⅞ in. deep. Cut the tenons on the braces to fit these mortises. Be careful to get the distance between the shoulders of the braces all of the same length. A good way to do this is to place them all side by side on a flat surface with the ends square and lay them all out at once. The top arms can be made in the same manner. The tenons should fit good and tight in all the posts.

The parts can now be glued and clamped together. When they are dry, scrape all the surplus glue from about the joints and go over the whole with fine sandpaper, removing all rough spots. Apply the finish you like best or the one that will match your other furniture. Purchase a few hooks at a hardware store and fasten in the upper arms as shown, and the hall tree is complete.

A TABLE FOR THE DEN

The table shown in the accompanying sketch is especially appropriate for the den; it might be used in any other part of the house as well. It may be built of plain-sawed red oak, or of quarter-sawed white oak. The wood should be thoroughly seasoned and devoid of imperfections.

Order the material as follows:

1 top piece, ¾ in. thick by 36 in. square, S-2-S.
4 legs, 2½ in. square by 30 in. long, S-4-S.
2 upper horizontals, 1⅛ by 2 by 36 in., S-4-S.
2 lower horizontals, ¾ by 2½ by 35 in., S-4-S.
4 keys, ½ by 1 by 5 in., S-2-S.

Lay out and cut the circular top first. Next cut the four legs to length. To get the slopes for the ends of the legs and the shoulders of the tenons, lay out a full-sized drawing in pencil and lay the bevel along these lines, adjusting the parts to the lines.

The top horizontals have grooves cut on either side to allow the posts to "set in." This is to give the frame more rigidity. The lower horizontals or stretchers are to be tenoned through the posts and keyed. That the keys may be alike in size, a good plan is to make them first, then make the mortises

Table Completed

in the stretchers to correspond. Work the keys to the proper thickness, unless they were ordered so, then to length and joint one edge straight and square. Next lay off across the key the lines A and B of the drawing so that A shall measure ½ in. and B ⅜ in. Draw a sloping line through these points

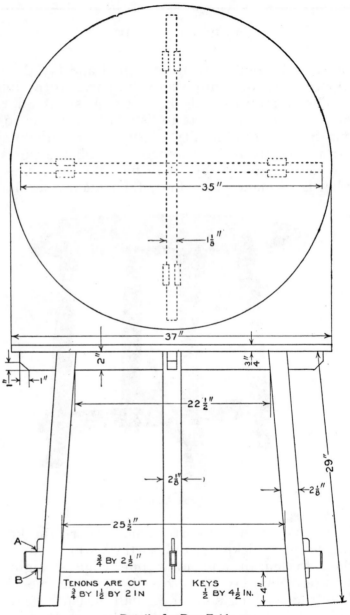

Detail of a Den Table

and work this edge of the key to size and shape. Round the top of the key as shown. Then mortise in the tenon, for the key can then be laid out to ½ in. for the top opening and ⅜ in. for the bottom.

The most satisfactory finish for mission designs, and the easiest to apply, is wax. It is an old finish that was superseded by varnish. Our ancestors used to make wax polish by "cutting" beeswax with turpentine. Cut up the beeswax and add to it about one-third its volume of turpentine. Heat to the boiling point in a double boiler. Or, melt a quantity of beeswax and to this add an equal volume of turpentine. Care must be taken that the turpentine shall not catch fire.

Rapid drying and hardening waxes can be purchased now-a-days. They require a smooth surface and a thin application for a successful result. Too much wax upon a rough surface will produce very ugly, white, chalk-like spottings as the wax dries. These are especially noticeable upon dark finishes. Waxes colored black overcome this, but are not necessary if the ordinary wax is properly applied. 1—Stain the wood, if a very dark finish is desired. 2—If the wood is coarse grained, put on one or two coats of paste filler and rub it off carefully, that a smooth surface may be prepared. Allow the stain 12 hours in which to dry, also each coat of filler. 3—With a soft cloth apply as thin a coating of wax as can be and still cover the wood. Wax is in paste form. 4—Allow this to stand five or ten minutes, then rub briskly with a soft dry cloth to polish. 5—Let stand 24 hours, then apply another coat.

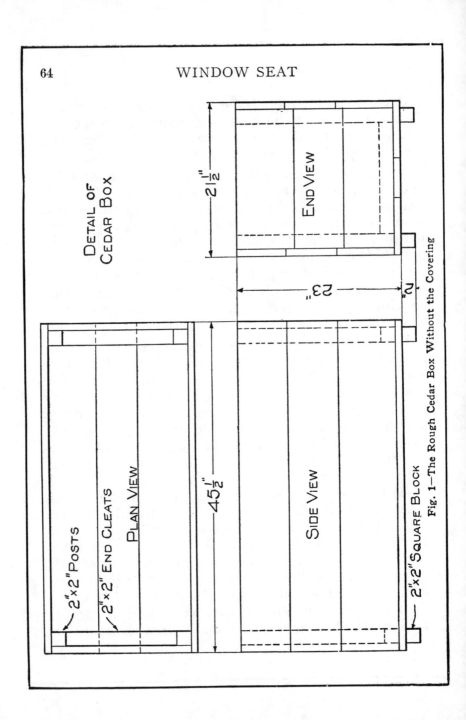

Fig. 1—The Rough Cedar Box Without the Covering

A BURLAP-COVERED WINDOW SEAT

A portable window seat of neat appearance, which is designed to take the place of a cedar chest, is shown in the accompanying sketch. If care is taken to make the joints fit well, the box will be practically airtight and mothproof, providing a place in which to store extra bedding or furs. The following list of materials will be needed:

36 ft. 1-in. thick cedar boards for the box.
1 piece pine, 2 by 2 in. by 12 ft. long.
32 ft. of ¼ by 2-in. oak strips.
54 ft. of ¼ by 1-in. oak strips.
16 doz. R. H. ¾-in. long brass screws.
1 piece green burlap, 24 by 48 in.
2 pieces green burlap, 20 by 44 in.
2 pieces green burlap, 20 by 20 in.
20 pieces red burlap, 3¼ in. square.

The box as shown in Fig. 1 is made first. Nail the sides and the bottom to the ends, being careful to get the box perfectly square. The corners can be dovetailed together if desired. The extra time it takes in making the dovetailed joints will greatly add to the durability of the box. The box can be made much stronger by nailing the sides and ends to posts 2 in. square placed on the inside. Cleats should also be placed on the inside, at the bottom, as shown. Fasten four blocks, 2 in. square, to the bottom for the box to rest upon. These can be attached with long screws run through from the bottom of the box.

The green burlap is glued to the outside of the box. Be careful not to apply too much glue on the burlap, or it will soak through. This should be tried out on a scrap piece, and when the proper application of glue is ascertained, applied to one side of the burlap and stuck on the box. Place the cloth on so

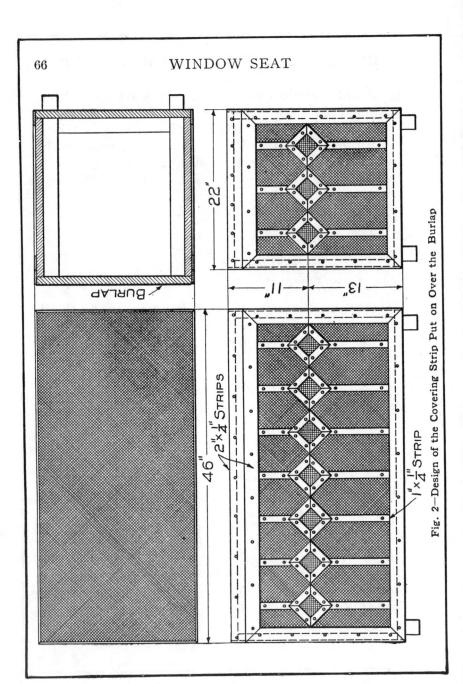

Fig. 2—Design of the Covering Strip Put on Over the Burlap

the weave will run in the same direction on all sides. The oak slats are cut and fit over the burlap as shown in Fig. 2. Care should be taken to make the mitered joints a tight fit. After the miters are all cut and the location of the squares found, they are marked so that pieces of red burlap may be placed over the green before the slats are fastened permanently. The slats are put in place over the burlap and fastened with small brass screws.

Cover the top or lid with green burlap, allowing the edges to lap over the ends and sides and fasten under the side strips. This top can be stuffed with excelsior, if desired, and tacks with large heads driven in to hold it in place. The slats can be stained any color to suit the maker. They should be removed from the box when being stained so as not to spot or stain the burlap.

QUARTER-SAWED OAK SETTEE

The mission settee shown in the accompanying picture should be made of quarter-sawed white oak. The material needed will be as follows:

4 posts, 3¼ by 3¼ by 36½ in., S-4-S.
4 end rails, 1½ by 5 by 32 in., S-4-S.
12 end slats, ⅝ by 3½ by 24 in., S-4-S.
1 front rail, 1½ by 7 by 87 in., S-4-S.
1 lower back rail, 1½ by 9 by 87 in., S-4-S.
1 upper back rail, 1½ by 12 by 87 in., S-4-S.
2 cleats for seat frame, 1½ by 2 by 82 in., S-4-S.
2 cleats for seat frame, 1½ by 2 by 32 in., S-4-S.

On account of the unusual width of the pieces that go into the makeup of this settee, it will be necessary to have the wood thoroughly seasoned before putting them together, otherwise shrinkage will cause them to crack open.

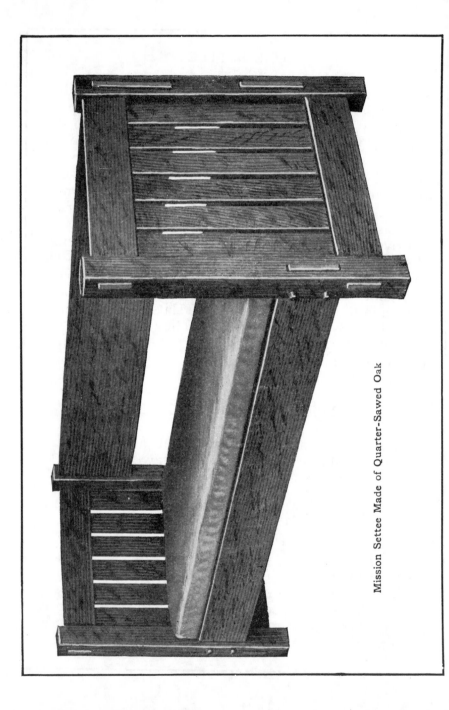

Mission Settee Made of Quarter-Sawed Oak

Begin work by making the ends of the settee first. Cut the posts to length, chamfering both top and bottoms somewhat so that they shall not splinter or cause injury to the hands. Next lay out and cut the mortises as shown on the drawing. With the posts finished, lay out the end rails, cutting the tenons and the mortises into which the ends of the slats are to be fitted.

It should be noted that the drawing calls for the "setting in" of the whole of the ends of the slats, there being no shoulders. This is much easier and gives just as satisfactory a result, provided the sides of the mortises are carefully cut.

Thoroughly scrape and sandpaper all these parts and then put the ends together. In addition to the glue it will be well to through pin each of the tenons and mortises. These pins may be put in flush and permanent on the ends of the settee. On the side rails, however, the pins are to be allowed to project so that they can be removed, and no glue is used in the joint.

While the glue of the ends is hardening, prepare the rails of front and back. Scrape and sandpaper these and when the clamps can be removed from the ends put the whole frame together. The ends of all projecting tenons are chamfered.

The illustration shows a loose leather cushion. There is quite a variety of materials out of which such a cushion can be made. The best, of course, is leather. In the highest class of furniture where loose cushions are used, the seat base is formed by solidly mortising a frame together on which is woven a heavy cane seating. This in turn is fastened to the inside of the piece of furniture, and the

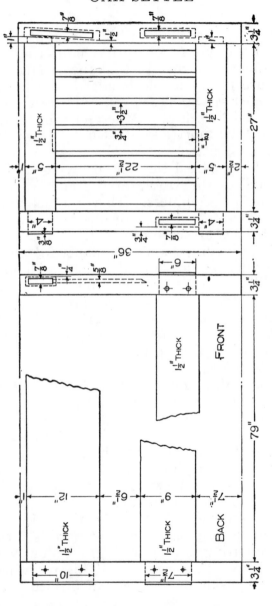

Detail of the Oak Settee

cushions when placed upon it make a very comfortable seat. The stock bill for this settee calls for such a frame. Wood slats may be substituted if desired.

This piece of furniture will look well if finished in weathered oak. See that all glue is removed from the surface, and that the wood is clean and smooth, and apply a coat of weathered oak oil stain. Sandpaper this lightly with No. 00 paper when the stain has thoroughly dried, and put on a coat of lackluster or an equivalent.

A SCREEN

In selecting or making up mission furniture for the home, a screen is necessary sometimes to add to the appearance of a room. The screen shown in the accompanying illustration consists of a few parts which are easily put together. The stock can be bought of any planing mill planed, sanded and cut to the proper lengths. The cloth, which should be of dark color, can be purchased at a dry goods store. The following list of material will be needed.

6 posts, 1 in. square by 65 in.
6 rails, ¾ in. square by 18 in.
6 rails, ½ in. square by 18 in.
3 panels, ¼ by 3 by 18 in.
6 yd. of cloth.
4 double-acting hinges.
2 doz. 2½-in. slender screws.

Cut or plow a groove ¼ in. wide and ¼ in. deep in the center of one surface on each of the ¾-in. rails. Cut out the ends with a compass saw. The five holes are bored with a 1-in. bit. The edges of these panels are inserted in the grooves of the ¾-in. rails, using plenty of good glue.

When the glue has dried for at least 24 hours the screen frame can be put together. Holes for the screws should be bored through the posts where the ¾-in. rails are joined and a screw turned into the end grain of each rail.

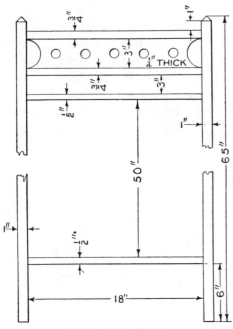

Detail of One Section

Scrape off all the surplus glue and sandpaper all the parts well. When this is done the finish can be applied. Any one of the mission stains can be used and finished with wax and polished.

The cloth is cut to length, a hem sewed on each end and one ½-in. rail put through each hem. Place the top rail in position and screw it fast. Stretch the cloth tight and fasten the lower ½-in. rail with screws at the bottom. Each section of the screen is finished in the same way.

The hinges are attached about 4 in. from each end of the posts in the same manner as hanging a door.

The sections can be made up in various ways to suit the builder. Instead of using cloth, heavy pasteboard, or board made up to take the place of plaster

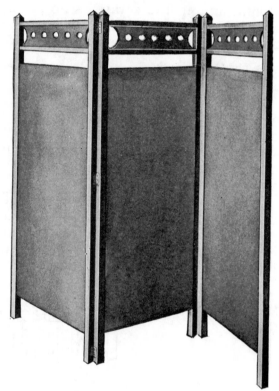

Screen of Three Sections

on walls of dwellings, may be substituted, thus forming a ground that will take paint and bronze decorations. A piece of this material can be easily cut to fit the opening in each section.

A MISSION BOOKRACK

The accompanying sketch shows a bookrack designed strictly along mission lines. Enough stock may be found among the scrap, as no piece is over 1 in. in width or thickness. If stock is not on hand, secure the following, cut to exact lengths:

2 stretchers, 1 by 1 by 20 in., S-4-S.
4 posts, 1 by 1 by 7½ in., S-4-S.
4 rails, 1 by 1 by 7 in., S-4-S.
8 slats, ½ by ½ by 3½ in., S-4-S.

Arrange the pieces as they are to be in the finished rack and number both parts of each joint. There will be twelve lap joints, and great care must be taken to mark them accurately and to cut to exactly half the depth of each piece.

First fit the posts and rails of the ends. To mark the width of each notch, lay the piece which is to fit into the notch upon it and thus get the exact size. Knife lines must be used for the width and light gauge lines for the depth of each notch.

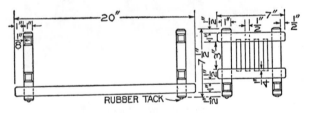

Detail of the Bookrack

Next lay out and cut joints between the stretchers and ends.

In each end there are four slats which should be

mortised into the rails ¼ in. Glue the pieces in place and clamp them with handscrews.

A rubber-headed tack in the bottom of each post will prevent the marring of the surface upon which the rack is to rest.

Mission, weathered or fumed-oak stain will look

The Complete Bookrack

well. A waxed finish should be used. Before applying the wax, it is well to use a very thin coat of shellac as a foundation. Let this coat stand for a few hours and allow an interval of at least an hour between applying the coats of wax.

Should the rack wind a little, it may be remedied by cutting off part of two diagonally opposite racks.

A ROUND EXTENSION DINING TABLE

This extension table should be made of some hard wood, preferably white oak. It will be a difficult matter to secure legs of the sizes indicated in solid pieces of clear stock. It will be possible, however,

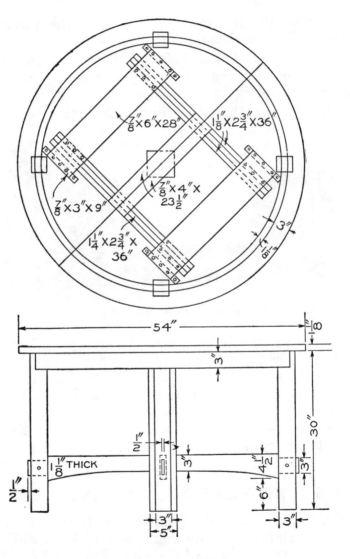

Detail of the Table

to secure them veneered upon white-pine cores. If the veneering is properly done these will serve the purpose very well, the lighter weight, due to the

Table for the Dining-Room Set

white-pine core, being an advantage. The circular facing is best made by first sawing a segment of the circle of the size wanted and then veneering the outer surface of this. Order the following stock:

4 legs, 3 by 3 by 30½ in., S-4-S.
1 leg, 5 by 5 by 30½ in., S-4-S.
4 rails, 1⅛ by 5 by 23 in., S-2-S.
4 facing segments, 1⅛ by 3¼ in. on a 24-in. radius.
1 top, 1⅛ in. thick on a 27-in. radius, S-2-S.
3 extra boards, 1⅛ by 12 by 55 in., S-2-S.
4 slides, 1⅛ by 2¾ by 36½ in., S-4-S, maple.
2 slides, 1¼ by 2¾ by 36½ in., S-4-S, maple.
4 frame pieces, ⅞ by 3 by 9 in., S-4-S, maple.
2 frame pieces, ⅞ by 6 by 28 in., S-4-S, maple.
2 frame pieces, ⅞ by 4 by 23½ in., S-4-S, maple.

There are various ways of arranging the slides to work one with the other. Several patented devices are on the market that permit a ready adjustment with but little effort and are used extensively by commercial manufacturers. The amateur will do well to secure a set before he undertakes to work these slides to shape.

Prepare the legs by cutting them to length. Lay out and work the mortises. The ends of the facings are to be tenoned and housed into the posts. Prepare the rails by cutting the tenons and shaping the lower edges as shown in the drawing. Prepare the top. After this, assemble this much of the frame, using plenty of clamps and good hot glue.

Next get the under frame and the slides ready and attach them as shown. There will be needed plenty of glue blocks for reinforcing the facing where it is fastened to the top, etc.

For a finish, apply a filler colored as desired. Upon this, after it has hardened and been sanded with No. 00 paper, apply a coat of shellac. Upon the shellac apply successively several coats of some good rubbing varnish. Rub the first coats with haircloth and the final coat with pulverized pumice and crude or linseed oil.

If an effect is wanted that will contrast, stain the wood first with a water stain. Sand this lightly when dry, then apply a second coat of stain diluted one-half with water. Again sand and then apply a thin coat of shellac. Sand this lightly, and apply the filler and the varnish as described above.

AN ARM DINING CHAIR

This armchair will look well if made of plain-sawed oak. Quarter-sawed oak might be used, or black walnut if desired. The stock bill specifies

Armchair of the Dining-Room Set

the various parts mill-planed to size as far as possible. If some amateur craftsman should prefer to do his own surfacing, thereby saving somewhat on the expense, he should add ¼ in. to the width of each piece, providing the stock is mill-planed to thickness. It is hardly profitable to get stock entirely in the rough if the work is to be done by hand. The following is the stock bill:

2 front posts, 1¾ by 1¾ by 25 in., S-4-S.
1 piece for back posts, 1¾ by 6 by 43 in., S-2-S.
2 arm pieces, ⅞ by 4 by 24½ in., S-4-S.
2 seat rails, 1 by 2½ by 22 in., S-4-S.
2 seat rails, 1 by 2½ by 24 in., S-4-S.
4 lower side rails, ⅝ by 1½ by 22 in., S-4-S.
2 front and back lower rails, ⅝ by 2¾ by 24 in., S-4-S.
1 back rail, ¾ by 2¼ by 24 in., S-4-S.
1 back rail, ¾ by 2½ by 24 in., S-4-S.
2 slats, ⅜ by 2 by 16½ in., S-4-S.
1 slat, ⅜ by 4½ by 16½ in., S-4-S.
2 braces, ⅞ by 2½ by 5½ in., S-2-S.

The design shown is for a chair in which the width of front and back is the same. Also the back leg parallels the front below the seat. In commercial practice the backs are usually made somewhat narrower than the fronts and the back leg is slanted somewhat below the seat as well as above. As this construction necessitates sloping shoulders on all tenons it complicates the problem when the work is not done by machinery. The ambitious amateur may readily get the proportion of slant by measuring common chairs. For mission effects the chair looks well with front and back the same width.

Prepare the front posts first and then the rear. The rear posts are to be cut from the single piece of stock specified. By proper planning both pieces may be gotten out without trouble. Lay off and cut the mortises.

Saw the rails to length and lay out and cut the tenons. The back rails are to have mortises in their edges to receive the ends of the slats. Instead of tenoning these slats make mortises large enough to receive the whole end—in other words, house the ends.

Shape the two arms, then glue up the back and then the front of the chair. After the glue has set sufficiently, assemble the remainder of the parts.

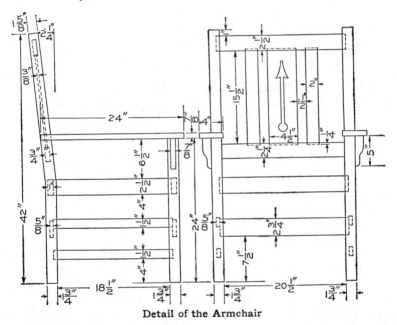

Detail of the Armchair

Thoroughly scrape and sandpaper the parts and then apply the finish.

For a seat, either a leather cushion may be placed upon slats or the bottom may be upholstered in the usual manner, using webbing on heavy canvas, and then felt or hair with a top of canvas and leather; the whole being firmly fastened with tacks and the leather with ornamental nails.

A HALL BENCH

All the stock for this bench should be of ⅞-in. oak, excepting the slats, which may be of a cheaper wood. The following list of lumber will be required to build it:

4 slats, ⅞ by 4 by 17 in., cheap wood.
2 cleats, ⅞ by 1 by 26 in., cheap wood.
4 end rails, ⅞ by 2 by 16¼ in., oak, S-2-S.
2 ends, ⅞ by 16 by 16¼ in., oak, S-2-S.
2 sides, ⅞ by 4 by 25 in., oak, S-2-S.
2 pieces, ⅞ by 5½ by 25 in., oak, S-2-S.

Start the work by first cutting the two pieces of ⅞ by 5½ by 25-in. material diagonally 1 in. from

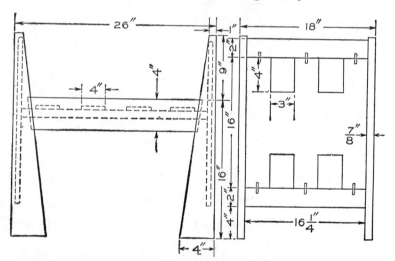

Detail of the Hall Bench

each corner, thus making the legs. The edges are planed square and the ends should be rounded a

little so that there will be no splinters projecting.
The legs are mortised 1 in. deep for the side rails.
The tenon ends are cut on the rails, care being
taken to get the right angle and a good fit. These

Bench Made of Plain Oak

can now be fastened together, using hot glue on
the entire surface of the joint.

While these are drying the ends can be made as
shown in the plan. The 3 by 4-in. holes are cut at
equal distances apart. Be sure that each end is perfectly square, then glue and dowel the 2-in. strips
at each end. The ends are then glued and nailed

to the sides, using finishing nails, which are set and the holes filled with colored putty.

The cleats are now fastened, extra care being taken when fastening them over the joints where the legs receive the side rails, as this will help to strengthen the joints. The slats rest on these cleats and are placed at equal distances apart.

The bench is now finished, but before applying the stain, see that all parts are free from glue and are well sandpapered.

The leather cushion should be the loose kind and of a shade to harmonize with the finish.

A SEWING TABLE

This convenient and useful table will be much appreciated by any woman. It has two drawers for sewing material, and two drop leaves to spread the work upon.

The following list of material will be needed for its construction. The sizes given are exact, so if the stock cannot be bought at a mill ready planed and squared, a slight allowance must be made for this.

4 posts, 1¼ by 1¼ by 27 in., S-4-S.
9 rails, ⅞ by 2 by 14½ in., S-2-S.
1 top, ⅞ by 18 by 18 in., S-2-S.
2 leaves, ⅞ by 10 by 18 in., S-2-S.
2 drawer fronts, ¾ by 5 by 13½ in., S-2-S.
4 drawer sides, ⅜ by 5 by 13 in., S-2-S.
2 drawer backs, ⅜ by 4⅛ by 13 in., S-2-S.
2 drawer bottoms, ⅜ by 12¾ by 13 in., S-2-S.
4 drawer slides, ⅞ by 2 by 13 in., S-2-S.
3 panels, ⅜ by 9⅜ by 14 in., S-2-S.
2 brackets, ⅞ by 3 by 4 in., S-2-S.

Have the surfaces of the legs exactly square with

each other. The ends must be square with all surfaces, but need not be planed smooth as neither will be seen in the finished table.

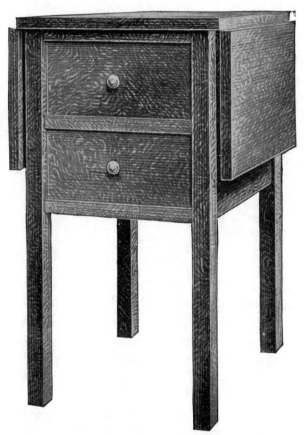

Sewing Table in Plain Oak

Arrange the rails in position. The two rails in each side and back are placed with the 2-in. surface out, while the three in the front have the 2-in. surface up for the drawers to slide upon. Mark the tenons, 1 in. by ⅜ in., with a knife and gauge lines on each end of the rails for the sides and back.

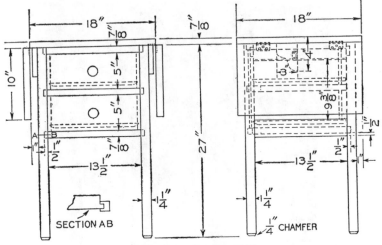

Detail of the Sewing Table

Mark the tenons, ¾ in. by ⅞ in., as shown in the sketch, on each end of front rails. Cut all the tenons with a backsaw and smooth them with a chisel.

Carefully mark the mortises in the legs, taking measurements for each mortise from the tenon which is to go into it. Fit together all rails and legs without glue to detect any errors.

See that the panels for sides and back are squared up true and the surfaces smooth. Mark the grooves for the panels in the side and back rails and legs. Cut the grooves with a chisel or plow plane to a depth of ¼ in.

Glue up the joints and clamp the two table sides

first. While the glue is setting, square up and smooth the top and two leaves perfectly.

Now glue up the whole table, having set in the front and back rails and panel. The drawer slides, two on each side, should next be put in. A nail through them and into each leg will hold them, as there is only the weight of the drawers resting on them. Fasten the top with screws through the rails from the under side. The leaves are attached with two 2-in. butt hinges which must be set in flush with the under surface to prevent a crack showing between the table top and leaf when the latter is raised. The small bracket hinged to the panel supports the open leaf.

The drawers are now made. Allow the side to lap over the front ½ in. as shown in sketch and fasten it with nails. The bottom should be let into

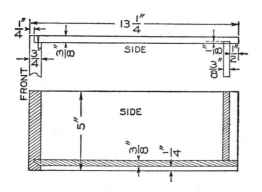

Construction of the Drawer

the sides and front ¼ in., but must not be nailed to them, because this would cause the drawer to stick, when the bottom expands.

Metal rings or wooden knobs will do well for the drawer pulls.

Stain to any desired shade and finish with a wax if a dull gloss is wanted, or with one coat of shellac and two coats of varnish for a highly polished surface.

A SIDE CHAIR

A companion piece to the chair with arms and the sideboard is the side chair illustrated herewith. It should be made of the same kind of wood and finished to correspond with the armchair. Order the following stock list:

```
2 front posts, 1½ by 1½ by 18½ in., S-4-S.
1 piece for back posts, 1½ by 5½ by 38½ in., S-2-S.
4 seat rails, 1 by 2 by 17 in., S-4-S.
4 lower side rails, ⅝ by 1¼ by 17 in., S-4-S.
2 lower front and back rails, ⅝ by 2½ by 17 in., S-4-S.
1 back rail, ¾ by 2¼ by 17 in., S-4-S.
1 back rail, ¾ by 2 by 17 in., S-4-S.
1 slat, ⅜ by 3 by 13½ in., S-4-S.
2 slats, ⅜ by 1½ by 13½ in., S-4-S.
```

Square up the front posts to length. From the single piece specified cut out the back posts, giving them the amount of slant indicated in the drawing. Set these four posts upright in the positions they are to occupy relative to one another in the finished piece, and mark off, as with penciled circles, the approximate locations of mortises. After this, lay them on the bench side by side, even the lower ends and locate accurately the ends of the mortises. Gauge their sides.

Saw the rails to length and lay out the shoulder lines and the cheeks of the tenons and cut them. Plan to house the ends of the slats in the back rails.

Side Chair of Dining-Room Set

While the drawing shows a chair in which the front and back are of equal width, the amateur may make the back narrower if he so desires. A

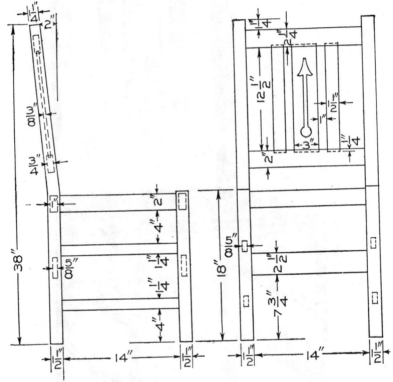

Detail of the Side Chair

measurement of a common chair will give the proportions.

Place the front and the back in the clamps and after the glue has had time to harden, assemble the remaining parts. Thoroughly scrape and sandpaper all the parts, carefully removing any surplus glue. Wood finish will not "take hold" where any glue has been allowed to remain.

The seat may be given the same treatment as suggested for the armchair. This should not be done, however, until the finish has been applied.

A simple finish is obtained by the application of a coat of paste filler of a soft brown color, if oak has been used. Apply and clean this off in the manner directed by the manufacturers and after it has had 24 hours in which to harden, sand it lightly with No. 00 paper. Over this apply a thin coat of shellac. Allow this to harden, then sandpaper lightly with fine paper. Upon the shellac apply several coats of some good rubbing wax. Follow the directions that are to be found upon the cans, being careful not to apply too much at a time. If too much wax is applied, it stays in the small pores of the wood and produces an ugly chalk-like appearance.

ANOTHER PIANO BENCH

The piano bench shown is best made of black walnut or oak and should be finished in the natural color for walnut, but stained some rich brown for oak.

The following pieces will be needed:

1 top, 1 by 15½ by 38½ in., S-2-S.
2 legs, 1 by 14½ by 20½ in., S-4-S.
2 rails, ⅞ by 3¾ by 36½ in., S-2-S.
1 stretcher, ¾ by 4¼ by 37 in., S-2-S.

The keys can be secured from the waste that will be cut off from the other parts.

Square up the top in the usual manner to the size indicated in the working drawing. In a similar manner square up the stretcher to width and length.

There will be no need to square the ends of the rails as they are to be cut off on a slant. Square up the sides or edges and then lay off and cut the slanting ends, smoothing them with the plane. Lay off and work the shape on their under edges.

The ends are best laid off by means of a template or pattern for which a piece of rather heavy paper will do. Lay off the main dimensions on a center line. Sketch in the curve of the edge after the slant has been laid out. Lay out the form at the bottom, then fold the paper along the center line and trace the other half. With this pattern lay off the outline upon the wood. For convenience in laying out

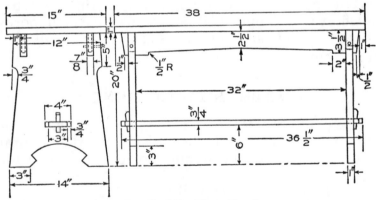

Detail of the Piano Bench

the grooves for the rails and the mortise for the tenon on the stretcher, it is well to work a face edge upon each leg and allow this to remain until these joints have been made and the parts fitted. The shape at the bottom of the leg is merely suggestive and may be modified as desired.

Lay out and work the tenons on the stretcher. Then lay out and work the grooves upon the rails. Each side of each rail is grooved ⅛ in. to allow the

Piano Bench
in Quarter-Sawed Oak

leg to be recessed. This is done to give the bench the bracing that is needed to make it stand firmly. Work the grooves in the legs and the mortises for the rails.

It should be noted that the mortise for the key in the stretcher must be laid out before the shoulders and cheeks of the tenon on which the mortise is made are cut off. Otherwise there would be no place to put the gauge in marking the sides of the mortise for the key.

Thoroughly scrape all the parts and then assemble them. No glue is needed. The rails are held in place by dowel pins, the heads of which are allowed to project slightly and rounded so as to give an ornamental effect. The top is attached by means of small angle irons or by means of blocks and screws fastened to the corners made by top and rails.

ANOTHER SCREEN

The screen shown in the accompanying illustration is made of burlap and plain-sawed oak. The stock list follows:

```
2 posts, 1½ by 1½ by 40 in., S-4-S.
2 base pieces, 3 by 3 by 12½ in., S-4-S.
2 horizontals, ¾ by 4¼ by 38 in., S-2-S.
1 horizontal, ¾ by 1½ by 38 in., S-2-S.
1 vertical, ¾ by 1¾ by 20 in., S-2-S.
4 braces, 1⅛ by 4¼ by 6½ in., S-2-S.
```

The two base pieces may be shaped first. The drawing shows the form and the dimensions. Make use of a face edge in laying out the mortises in the base pieces for the uprights, before these face edges are removed to make the slanting sides.

Work the verticals to length, laying out and cutting the tenons at the bottoms, and shaping the tops as shown.

Lay out and shape the three horizontals as shown, working the tenons upon the ends of each and the mortises in the lower two for the tenons of the middle vertical.

For the braces, secure a face edge on each piece and square one end of each to that. Lay off the curve free-hand upon one block and cut it out. Use this block as a pattern or template to lay off the others.

Thoroughly scrape and sandpaper all the parts,

then assemble them, using clamps and good hot glue. Take care to see that there is no warp in the frame as it lies in the clamps. After the glue on the frame has hardened, remove the clamps and attach

Plain-Oak Frame with
Burlap Panels

the base blocks and the braces. The braces are secured by means of round-head screws.

Remove the surplus glue and then apply a finish as desired.

For the paneling, frames will be needed about which to fasten the burlap. These may be made of

½-in. soft wood and the following pieces will be necessary:

    2 pieces, ½ by 2 by 36 in., S-2-S.
    2 pieces, ½ by 2 by 8 in., S-2-S.
    4 pieces, ½ by 2 by 18 in., S-2-S.
    4 pieces, ½ by 2 by 19 in., S-2-S.

Make these frames enough smaller than the openings they are to occupy to allow for burlap and

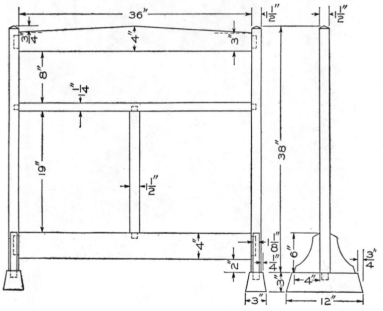

Detail of the Frame

tacks. These frames are held in place by putting fixed nails in the top of each frame before the burlap is attached. Holes are bored in the rails to correspond to them. The lower edges of the frames are held in place by nails inserted up through the rails upon which the frames rest.

A FOLDING CARD TABLE

The accompanying sketch shows the details of a card table that can be folded up and carried about or stored away when not in use. We would advise making two tables at the same time, as the material for both can be purchased nearly as cheaply as for one. The material necessary for making one table is given in the following list:

1 piece, 7/8 by 1 3/16 by 27 1/2 in., basswood or poplar.
2 pieces, 7/8 by 1 3/16 by 29 1/4 in., basswood or poplar.
4 legs, 1 in. square, 24 3/4 in. long; oak.
4 pieces, 1 in. square, 5 in. long; oak.
4 side pieces, 3/8 by 1 3/8 by 29 5/8 in.; oak.
4 pieces, 27 1/2 in. long, single groove electric wire moulding with batten.
1 piece cardboard, 1/8 in. thick, 29 1/4 in. square.
4 pieces brass rod, 3/16 in. diameter, 15 in. long.
30 small copper washers, 3/8 or 7/16 in. outside diameter and drilled 3/16 in.
4 brass corners, 1 3/8 in. deep.
2 1/2 doz. No. 5 oval head brass screws, 3/4 in. long.
4 No. 2, 7/8-in. rubber screw tips.
1 piece felt, 1 yd. square.
1 sheet wadding, 1 yd. square (if pad is wanted under felt).
1 pt. wood stain.
3 doz. No. 14 wire beads, 2 in. long.
Some 2-oz., 4-oz., and 6-oz. flat-head tacks.

Begin by squaring up the four legs making them all 24 3/4 in. long and 1 in. square. Also square up the crosspieces marked B in the detail drawing. These should be 5 in. long and should have 1/4-in. holes about 1 in. deep drilled in both ends of each for the 1/4-in. oak swivel pins. Measure back 1 1/2 in. from one end of each and bore a 9/16-in. hole, 7/8 in. deep as shown. Now cut a tenon on one end of each leg, 3/4 in. long, that will fit tightly in this 9/16-in. hole. Round the corners of the piece B at the top as shown at C. Fasten the two pieces together with glue and brads, being careful to get them

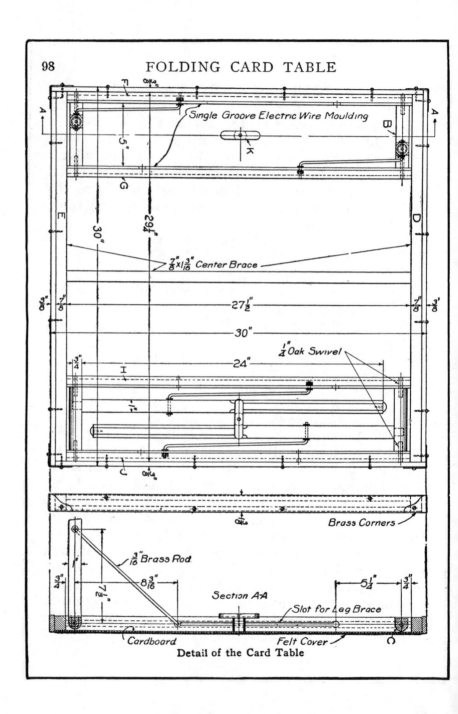

Detail of the Card Table

square with each other. After the glue is set bore a $\frac{3}{16}$-in. hole in the center of the leg, 7 in. from the edge of the crosspiece, for the brace rod. Bevel the corners as shown. Sandpaper them smooth, then stain and polish.

Lay the two pieces marked D and E in the sketch on a level surface with the $\frac{7}{8}$-in. edge up, place the

Card Table Ready for Use

cardboard on top and tack it fast to the pieces, using 6-oz. tacks. Place the center piece in and tack it fast also. Fasten the ends to the other pieces with brads. The four pieces of electric wire moulding should each measure exactly $27\frac{1}{2}$ in. long, or the same length as the center piece. Fit a piece of wood about 4 in. long in the groove at each end of the moulding, plane down and fasten with brads. Next take the thin batten or covering strip that comes with the moulding and bore a ½-in. hole in the center, 6 in. from one end, and a ¼-in. hole, $8\frac{3}{16}$ in. from the other end. With a gouge cut a slot ¼ in. wide from one hole to the other in the center as shown in the section A-A. Sandpaper this slot smooth and then fasten the batten to the moulding with small brads driven in about 2 in. apart. At a point ¾ in. from each end and in the center drill ¼-in. holes through the moulding at the small ends of the slots. These are for the ends of the brace rods to spring into, to lock the legs when they are open. Tack the two pieces of moulding marked F and J on the remaining edges of the cardboard with the slots facing in and the large holes of the slots at opposite sides, then place the other two pieces (G and H) 5 in. inside of these, or just the length of the cross ends of the legs, with the slots facing the first two placed (F and J) and tack fast with 4-oz. tacks. Use brads at the ends and be careful that they do not enter the ¼-in. holes. This part of the table can now be stained or painted the same as the legs. The ⅜-in. side pieces can also be stained at this time.

The ends of the brass rods can be bent in a vise. One end should be 1 in. long and should be square with the stock. Measure 11¼ in. center to center and bend in opposite direction, leaving this end at a slight angle out from square. Just at this bend raise a burr with a sharp chisel to keep the washer on. Now place five of the copper washers on the 1-in. end and batter the end of the rod so they will not slip off. They should be loose so that they will roll and slip on the brace. Slip a washer on the other end and put the end of the rod through the $\frac{3}{16}$-in. hole in the leg from the short end side, place another washer on the rod, saw off and rivet down the end.

To put the legs in the table, slip the end of one of the braces and the washers in the large hole in

The Legs Fold on the Under Side of Top

the slot, shove it up until the ¼-in. hole in the crosspiece and the one in the moulding meet, then drive an oak dowel or rod into each end. This is the hinge or pivot that the legs swing on. When the leg is extended the end of the brace rod should spring into the ¼-in. hole in the moulding and lock the leg in place. Rubber tips should be put on the bottom ends of the legs. Two wooden buttons should be made and fastened to the cardboard as shown at K for locking the legs when they are closed.

The felt can now be put on the top of the table. Stretch it tightly and then tack the edges securely to the sides of the table. Now fasten on the ⅜-in. side pieces and the brass corners with the small brass screws as shown on the drawing, and the table is complete.

MAGAZINE STAND

If you do not possess the necessary tools for getting out the material used in this piece of furniture, it can be purchased from a mill already planed, sanded and cut to lengths given in the list. Any kind of wood can be used, but quarter-sawed red oak with a mission stain and waxed, gives the best appearance. The following pieces will be needed:

2 shelves, ⅜ by 8 by 15 in., S-2-S.
1 shelf, ⅜ by 10 by 15 in., S-2-S.
1 shelf, ⅜ by 12 by 15 in., S-2-S.
8 slats, ⅜ by 1⅛ by 38 in., S-4-S.
2 slats, ¼ by 1⅛ by 38 in., S-4-S.
4 doz. 1 in. No. 9 round-head screws.

Take the four shelves and line them up with their backs and ends even and clamp them together firmly. Mark the places for the slats across the edges of the shelves, making the first line ½ in. from their ends. Use a square to get the lines at right angles to the surface. Another line is drawn 1⅛ in. from the first, or the width of the slat. The ends of the shelves are marked in the same manner, beginning from the back edges and making the first line ½ in. from them, and then another line 1⅛ in. from the first, or the width of the slat. Make a line across the ends,

Stand Complete

½ in. from the front edge of the 8-in. shelves, and
another line 1⅛ in. back from the first one.   This
will leave 2½ in. and 4½ in. of space respectively
from the front edges of the 10-in. and 12-in. shelves.

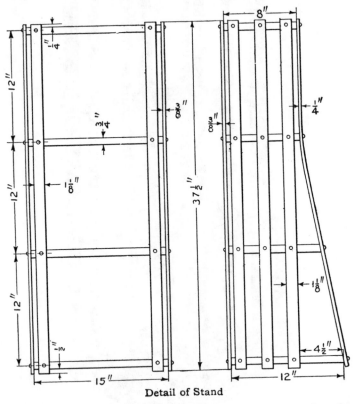

Detail of Stand

Shift the shelves so they will be even on the front
edges and mark them the same as the back.   Make
a ¼-in. depth mark on all edges between the lines
and cut this material out.   This can be done while
the shelves are clamped together.

Place the shelves on end in their order and start by screwing on the back slats on both ends first, then screw on the two front slats. Turn the stand down and put on the two back slats. Attach the two front slats on the top shelf first. Then bore the places for the remaining holes and turn in the screws. This will bend the slats into place. The two remaining slats are screwed on the ends of the shelves without letting them in, making the spaces equal. Mark each slat ½ in. below the bottom shelf and saw them off. The stand can be taken apart, sandpapered and stained.

A TABOURET

The stock necessary to make a tabouret of craftsman design as shown in the accompanying illustration can be purchased from the mill ready cut to length, squared and sanded. Quarter-sawed oak is the best wood to use and it is also the easiest to secure. Order the following pieces:

4 legs, 1½ in. square by 22 in. long.
1 top, ¾ in. thick by 14 in. square.
4 top rails, ¾ by 4 by 12 in.
4 lower rails, ¾ by 3 by 12 in.

First square up the four legs. Bevel the tops at an angle of 30 deg. and hollow out the lower part of the legs as shown in the detail sketch. Clamp them together with the ends square and lay out the mortises all at once. Cut the tenons on the rails to fit these mortises. Lay them out in the same manner as the posts so as to get them all the same distance between shoulders. The upper rails should be cut out underneath as shown.

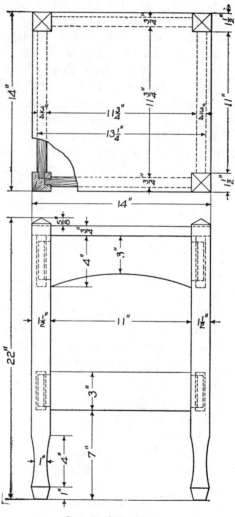

Detail of Tabouret

The rails and posts can now be glued together. Be careful to get them joined perfectly square. When they are dry cut and fit the top as shown. This is fastened to the top rails by means of screws

Finished Tabouret

from the inside. Remove all surplus glue from about the joints, as the finish will not take where there is any glue. Go over the whole with fine sandpaper and remove all rough spots, then apply the finish you like best.

Complete Porch Swing

A PORCH SWING

The porch swing shown in the illustration can be made of southern pine at a very moderate cost. It should be suspended by rustless black chains and eyebolts passing through the lower rails. If cushions are desired they can be made up quite cheaply of elastic felt covered with denim cloth.

These pieces, dressed and sanded, may be bought at the mill:

```
2 rails, 1¾ by 3 by 71 in., S-4-S.
1 rail, 1¾ by 3 by 65 in., S-4-S.
2 posts, 1¾ by 3 by 25 in., S-4-S.
2 posts, 1¾ by 3 by 17 in., S-4-S.
2 rails, 1¾ by 3 by 22½ in., S-2-S.
2 arm rests, ⅞ by 4 by 28 in., S-2-S.
5 slats, ⅜ by 5 by 16 in., S-2-S.
8 ft. flooring for bottom.
2 cleats, ⅞ by 1½ by 57 in., S-4-S.
```

Plane and square the ends of all the rails and posts. Lay out the lap joints for the back rails and posts. Use a knife line for this and saw exactly to the line to avoid trimming with the chisel. When sawing be careful to cut exactly halfway through the thickness of each piece. In the same way make the lap joints between the front rail and posts. Have the two end rails exactly the same length and proceed to fasten the front and back posts to them, using 4-in. lag screws and washers. Bore through the posts and part way into the ends of the end rails for the lag screws.

The slats are mortised ½ in. into the back rails, or a ⅜-in. groove may be planed in these rails, the entire distance between joints, to receive the slats. A rabbeting plane will be needed for this. The arm rests lap over the back posts and are held to them

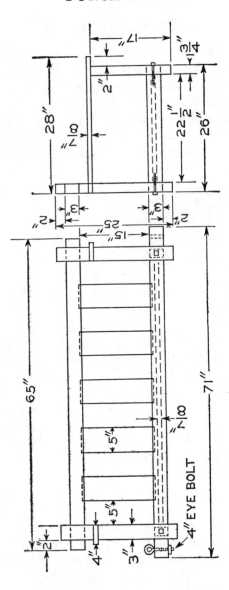

Detail of the Porch Swing

with 2-in. round-head screws. They may be fastened to the top of the front posts with round-head screws or dowel pins.

Ordinary pine flooring makes a good, tight seat, or ⅞-in. board may be used if desired. Fasten the cleats, which support the seat, to the front and back lower rails with 1½-in. screws.

To bring out the beautiful grain of southern pine, stain it brown or black and finish with two coats of waterproof varnish.

A FOOT WARMER

This foot warmer is so constructed that two bricks may be heated and placed inside of the stool.

Oak is the most suitable wood to use, and the following pieces will be needed:

4 legs, 1¼ by 1¼ by 8 in., S-4-S.
4 side rails, ⅞ by 3 by 8½ in., S-2-S.
4 top pieces, ⅞ by 1½ by 12 in., S-2-S.
1 bottom piece, ⅞ by 8½ by 8½ in., S-2-S.
1 piece asbestos, 8½ by 8½ in.
4 pieces asbestos, 2 by 8½ in.
1 sheet of brass, 13 by 13 in., 17 gauge.
2 hinges, 1 elbow catch, 3 doz. ornamental tacks.

The work may be started by shaping the four legs and cutting the mortises for the rails. Tenons are cut on the ends of the rails to fit in the mortises made in the posts. They are then glued together, care being taken to get the stool perfectly square.

The top frame can now be made and covered with the sheet of brass. The frame has mitered corners and the inside of the frame must be even with the inside of the rails. This in turn is fastened to the stool with the two hinges on the back and the elbow catch on the front side to keep it closed.

The design on the brass can be made by tacking

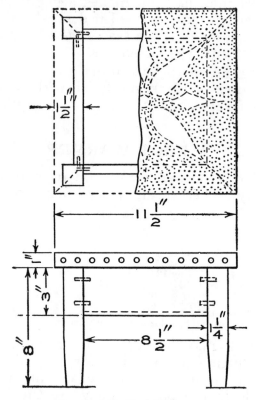

Detail of the Foot Warmer

it on a board, laying out the design and piercing the background with some sharp-pointed tool. This leaves the design raised with a smooth surface.

The brass can now be removed from the board,

placed on the frame and fastened with the ornamental tacks.

Turn the stool bottom side up and line the inside of the rails with asbestos; then place the bricks

Oak Stool with Brass Cover

on the inside of the stool. Both should fit up tight to the brass when the bottom is in place.

The stool is now ready for the finish, which can be of some stain to match the other furniture in the room where it is to be used.

A PLATE RACK FOR THE DINING ROOM

This plate rack can be made of any kind of wood and finished to match other pieces of furniture in the room, but as it is of mission design, oak is the most suitable lumber, as it takes the mission stain so nicely.

The material required is as follows:

4 posts, 1½ by 1½ by 28 in., S-4-S.
1 top, ⅞ by 7¼ by 48 in., S-2-S.
2 plate rails, ⅞ by 6¼ by 32 in., S-2-S.
2 back boards, ⅞ by 7¼ by 25 in., S-2-S.
2 side boards, ⅞ by 5¼ by 25 in., S-2-S.
4 shelves, ⅞ by 6½ by 8¼ in., S-2-S.
2 plate rests, ⅞ by ⅞ by 32 in., S-4-S.

This stock is specified to exact thickness, but some

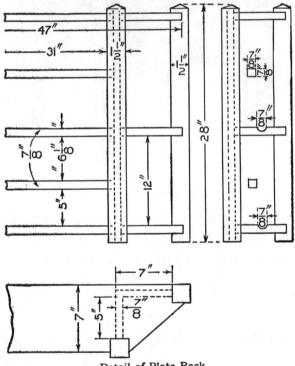

Detail of Plate Rack

allowance is made for trimming on the edges and
ends.

Begin work by squaring up the posts to length
and beveling the top ends, then trim the back and

side boards. These are nailed together, lapping the
back board over the side board. The posts are fastened with dowels placed at equal distances apart.
Hot glue is used in the joints.

The four shelves are now put in place. These

Dining-Room Plate Rack

are notched out to fit around the posts and are
nailed and glued.

While the glue is hardening on these, the plate
rails can be cut. These have $7/8$-in grooves near the
front edge to receive the lower edge of the plates
when resting against the two strips placed 5 in.
above the plate rails and far enough back to prevent
the plates from falling forward.

The rails are fastened to the two sides with dowels, three at each end being sufficient. The two strips fit in mortises cut in the side pieces. The top is then put on. This fits around the posts and rests on the sides. Hooks on which to hang cups are placed under the rails. All parts are thoroughly sandpapered before the stain is applied.

A MISSION SIDEBOARD

The sideboard is a piece designed to go with the armchair and side chair with similar paneling design. Like these chairs the sideboard should be

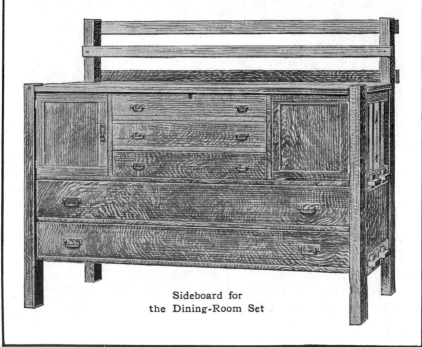

**Sideboard for
the Dining-Room Set**

made of hard wood and should be similarly finished. The drawer pulls, if not made of wood, should be of such metal and design as to harmonize with the mission style. Wrought-iron effects in plain outlines are appropriate.

Drawer sides, bottoms and backs may be made of some soft wood, such as yellow poplar. The small top drawer may be lined with ooze leather for holding silverware.

Obtain the following stock:

```
2 posts, 2 by 2 by 50 in., S-4-S.
2 posts, 2 by 2 by 39 in., S-4-S.
1 top, 1 by 23 by 58 in., S-2-S.
2 plate rails, ½ by 2 by 58 in., S-4-S.
1 plate rail, ½ by 1½ by 58 in., S-4-S.
2 rails, ⅞ by 2 by 21 in., S-4-S.
2 rails, ⅞ by 2½ by 21 in., S-4-S.
2 rails, ⅞ by 3 by 21 in., S-4-S.
4 slats, ⅜ by 1½ by 10½ in., S-4-S.
2 slats, ⅜ by 3½ by 10½ in., S-4-S.
2 panels, ⅜ by 18¾ by 10 in., S-2-S.
1 back rail, ⅞ by 2 by 54 in., S-4-S.
1 back rail, ⅞ by 3⅛ by 54 in., S-4-S.
1 back rail, ⅞ by 3 by 54 in., S-4-S.
2 back stiles, ⅞ by 1¾ by 11 in., S-4-S.
2 back stiles, ⅞ by 2½ by 11 in., S-4-S.
1 back panel, ⅜ by 10 by 24½ in., S-2-S.
1 back panel, ⅜ by 11½ by 53 in., S-2-S.
2 back panels, ⅜ by 11 by 11 in., S-2-S.
1 drawer front, ¾ by 3 by 24½ in., S-4-S.
2 drawer fronts, ¾ by 4 by 24½ in., S-4-S.
2 drawer fronts, ¾ by 6 by 52½ in., S-4-S.
2 drawer ends, ½ by 3 by 20 in., S-4-S, poplar.
4 drawer ends, ½ by 4 by 20 in., S-4-S, poplar.
4 drawer ends, ⅝ by 6 by 20 in., S-4-S, poplar.
3 drawer backs, ⅜ by 4 by 24 in., S-2-S, poplar.
2 drawer backs, ⅜ by 6 by 52 in., S-2-S, poplar.
3 drawer bottoms, ⅜ by 20 by 24 in., S-2-S, poplar.
2 drawer bottoms, ⅜ by 20 by 52 in., S-2-S, poplar.
2 drawer supports, ¾ by 2½ by 24½ in., S-4-S.
4 drawer supports, ¾ by 2½ by 54 in., S-4-S.
10 drawer slides, ¾ by 2 by 22 in., S-4-S.
2 middle verticals, ¾ by 22 by 13 in., S-2-S.
Drawer guides can be made from scrap stock.
```

A detailed description is hardly necessary for such a piece of work as this. Anyone capable of building it, will know the order of the different operations that are required in its construction.

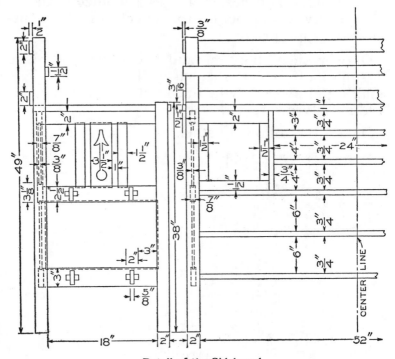

Detail of the Sideboard

It may be said that the two back panels at either side of the small drawers may be filled with beveled plate glass instead of wood if one so choose.

CONTENTS

120   CONTENTS